thanks for your kindness,
Hugh Oct 2012

CRUISE TO CAPE TOWN

A journey into a new South Africa

by

Hugh Leggatt

Grosvenor House
Publishing Limited

Hugh Leggatt is hereby identified as author of this
work in accordance with Section 77 of the Copyright, Designs
and Patents Act 1988

The book cover picture is copyright to Hugh Leggatt

This book is published by
Grosvenor House Publishing Ltd
28-30 High Street, Guildford, Surrey, GU1 3EL.
www.grosvenorhousepublishing.co.uk

A CIP record for this book
is available from the British Library

ISBN 978-1-78148-537-8

Dedication

For Susan, Guy, Lucy and Roger

Contents

First words

"Others feel the sweetness of contentment and well-being; I feel it just as much as they do, but not by letting it just slip away. Rather I seek to study it, reflect on it and savour it, in order to be able to render just thanks to him by whom it has been accorded."

—-Montaigne, *Essays* III. Ch. XIII

Quoted by Harold Nicolson in the preface to his 1957 book *Journey to Java*.

On the occasion of his 70th birthday in 1956, Harold Nicolson – diarist, diplomat and politician – was "the recipient of an enormous cheque" from 255 of his friends. He decided to spend it on a visit to the Far East with his wife, the famed writer and gardener Vita Sackville-West. They sailed from England on the Dutch ship MV *Willem Ruys* on 15 January 1957 and returned on 17 March, "two of the happiest months which, in a life of wholly unmerited felicity, I have ever enjoyed".

After the trip he wrote a book about it, *Journey to Java*, a record that is not only interesting for the descriptions of the ship, the voyage and the passengers but also for the philosophic digressions of the writer, often inspired by the books he was reading during the voyage.

Fifty years later, in 2006, I sailed with my wife Susan on Cunard's RMS *Queen Mary 2* from Southampton to New York. While I revelled in shipboard life, Susan was not so sure. Then, in October 2010, I received a booklet from Cunard offering a *QM2* world voyage in January 2012 with the first leg going to Cape Town. It was a voyage I had always wanted to make – Southampton to Cape Town, the route of the Union Castle ships that were once the staple of travel between South Africa and England. With Susan still working, it made sense for me to take the cruise and she would join me by air for a holiday at the Cape, seeing family and friends, before flying home together.

And I had Harold Nicolson as my inspiration and mentor: I too would write a diary of descriptions, impressions and reminiscences, following the daily entry format of *Journey to Java*. And so we did it; I sailed on 10 January 2012 and disembarked at the Cape 15 days later on 24 January. Susan joined me on 29 January and we flew home on 13 February.

I am no Nicolson of course, neither in ability, learning nor background. I'm a Canadian and British citizen with South African roots. I spent the first 35 years of my life in South Africa, 13 of them as a reporter on the largest circulation daily newspaper, *The Star*, before emigrating to Canada. I forfeited citizenship of the apartheid state when I took Canadian citizenship in 1984. I am British by virtue of my father – whose family background is discussed in these pages – who was born outside Birmingham. So I am rather a mongrel when it comes to nationality and allegiance.

My British-born wife Susan and I emigrated from Cape Town to Vancouver in 1980 with two young children, Guy and Lucy, aged seven and four, and a year later added another son, Roger. I was briefly a reporter with the *Vancouver Province* before landing a job with a mining company as a public relations officer. For 20 years in Vancouver I enjoyed the role of an in-house editorial and information specialist with two of Canada's largest international mining firms. In 2000 I took advantage of an opportunity in London with Rio Tinto, a global mining company, and for the second time embarked on a new life, perhaps more stimulating than Vancouver but certainly less carefree.

Though never brilliant, his work is always satisfactory, my headmaster wrote of me in a letter of reference when I left school. For a person endowed with average gifts, rash impulses and no inclination for a Plan B, I have pushed my luck and been lucky. Echoing Harold Nicolson's "happiest months" verdict, I can truly say my cruise on the famous liner and stay at the Cape added further relish to a lifetime of satisfaction. To my family I say, if you want to know what Dad did on his holiday, read the book.

Hugh Leggatt
21 February 2012

Chapter 1

Madeira

Tuesday 10 January

Embarkation, Southampton

Fifteen months after deciding to go, I was going. It had been a long wait but now I was off. At our home in Farnham in Surrey, the taxi arrives early as Steve, the driver, is concerned about roadworks around Southampton. S is tearful when we embrace and say goodbye. I think she suddenly envies me going, but in less than three weeks' time she will be flying out to join me.

Outside the car window as we head for the coast and Southampton, the lush Hampshire countryside matches my good mood; a beautiful and serene tapestry of hedges, mounded fields and patches of woodland, slumbering green in the weak winter sunshine.

1

We are soon there. The city where three rivers flow into a protected inlet, with "double tides" giving several hours a day of rising water, has long been England's shipping gateway to the ocean and the wide world beyond. It is the perfect place to catch a ship, and you can't miss the *Queen Mary 2*, even though it takes Steve's satnav to pinpoint which dock, the Ocean Cruise Terminal. A gatekeeper directs us to a lane where Steve stops and unloads my case. A man with a hand truck and wearing a bib with "Solent Stevedores" takes over, saying "It all comes with the service".

I find it is rather early for check in as Steve has delivered me one full hour ahead of time. I had heard that the Cunard line had decided to change the port of registration of their ships from Southampton to Bermuda because of European Union employment conditions imposed on British registered ships. It had something to do with pay differentials between the officer class (mainly British) and the crew (mainly Filipino).

I walk down the dock behind the terminal building to see for myself the register of this ship posing as a British icon in the tradition of Drake, Cook and the *Titanic*, but constructed in France, owned by the Americans and now registered in Bermuda.

Here at the back is the Land of Logistics. Behind a tall wire fence, the delivery of stores for the ship is going on through the back door. Near the stern are piled pallets of food: boxes of melons from Brazil, crates of potatoes from Lincolnshire and leeks and lettuce from the

Netherlands. I reach the back of the ship, towering above me like a 15 storey building. And there it is across the stern in white lettering: Queen Mary 2 Hamilton (Hamilton being the capital of tax haven Bermuda). I suppose it is a bit British because it is a colony, famously governed during the Second World War by the disgraced Duke of Windsor after his abdication as Edward VIII.

Standing there where no passengers are expected to go, at my feet discarded coils of hawser ropes and other maritime junk, as well as tugs waiting alongside apparently unmanned, I take some pictures, then go back to join the conventional tourists.

The terminal is not as crowded as expected. It is so well organised that queues are short. The terminal is new, having only opened in 2009. I am given a red card E, a form to fill in to say I do not have a cold or a tummy bug, and told to wait until group E is called. There are good views of the ship alongside, a massive motionless bulk looming over us, painted charcoal grey with white topsides, the ultimate in marine engineering and one of the biggest cruise ships afloat. It is really huge, too much to take in at close quarters. It is said to be longer than the Eiffel Tower is tall.

When group E is called, the check-in is quick. The e-ticket I printed at home is given hardly a glance but my British passport is closely scrutinised. They take a picture of me and this is embedded in the bar code of a card so that when it is swiped my picture and details come up on the screen of the operator. Security before boarding is like at an airport, complete with taking laptops out separately. Some people have to take off their shoes.

I am welcomed at the top of the gangway and cross the luxuriously carpeted and panelled Grand Lobby to the lift and find my cabin in the front part of the ship on Deck 12 quite easily. There is my case standing at the door in welcome. I booked an inside cabin. These are placed in bays off the main corridor so that entrance doors don't open opposite one another. The outside sea view cabins on Deck 12 must be the expensive ones. My cabin, 12011, which they call a "stateroom", looks small but everything is ship-shape and clean, with a large double bed and more cupboard space than I need. A leather apron is spread on the bed to put your case on to protect the linen while you unpack.

On the table by way of greeting is a complimentary bottle of Pol Acker sparkling wine in an ice bucket all chilled with napkin over and ready to go. I pour myself a glass to sip while I unpack. I stow all my gear in drawers and wardrobes. My steward calls to introduce himself. His name is Dong and he comes from Manila. He explains the arrangements for collecting laundry and tells me I should go to Deck 7 at 4pm for the safety drill.

My cabin is beige with sleek blonde wood doors and fittings. There is a phone to call the steward or make a satellite call. Although there is no window or outside aspect I do not find this a problem, in fact it makes it quite cosy. The air conditioning is efficient and obedient to manual setting of the thermostat and the desk is comfortable for writing (as long as I don't look up and see myself in the mirror). The British style electrical outlets below the mirror are handy for re-charging my mobile phone, computer and camera battery.

Fortified by the wine, I put on my fleece top and go on deck for the first time: one level up to Deck 13 which is the sundeck. It is so easy to get to it, just like going out on the patio. But this is a massive patio with huge wide games decks, a bar (not open) and tables and piles of loungers not set up yet. I do the tour, having a look and taking pictures with the backdrop of Southampton Water and the gloomy industrial shoreline. I go down in the elevator to Deck 7 to check out the all day buffet called King's Court, and from the promenade deck watch the loading operations at dockside: the dance of the forklift trucks.

While I am watching a man who is on his own suddenly exclaims and shows me the back of his jacket which he has taken off in disgust. A seagull has deposited a large dollop of white dropping down the back of his jacket. I look up and there are the guilty gull bombers circling overhead. I commiserate with the fellow and he gallantly takes the view that it is lucky it was not on his head.

The forklift trucks have hydraulic extension arms which pick up pallets of goods one by one to deliver them into the ship at dock level. Probably the stevedore company gets penalised financially if it does not load on time because a grey haired supervisor is pacing about in agitation raising his voice to the operators and waving his arms.

There is a lot to load but they seem to have enough time even though the ship docked from New York only this morning. For an asset that cost $800 million, the meter is running all the time. She must keep moving to pay her way. The logistics of resupplying between voyages is amazing – what, how much of it and where from.

I go down to the safety briefing far too early and feel a bit foolish carrying my bulky orange lifejacket. I ask around and they say the briefing is at 4.30pm not 4pm, and eventually an announcement says it will be at 5pm. I find my muster station for Section B which is in the Winter Garden restaurant in the forward part of Deck 7. Crew with colourful baseball caps and wearing their lifejackets are on hand to supervise us. I think it must be straight forward but I put my lifejacket on back to front and have to be corrected. One of the crew says he is on board employed as a singer so it seems they make their entertainers do double duty in passenger relations.

The briefing is given over the loudspeaker by the Commodore, the chief commanding officer of the ship, in a measured, clearly enunciated British voice. Later I hear he is a New Zealander. Seven short blasts and one long one means drop everything, go to your stateroom to fetch your lifejacket and "medication" (stayin' alive pills?) and go to your muster station. The alarm is not a signal to abandon ship, says the Commodore. You will be told what to do next: the order to abandon ship will come only from the bridge, in the unlikely event it is necessary. Eventually our muster station announcer says the drill is over and our holiday can start. Cheers all round.

I go back to my cabin and then up to Deck 13 for departure. I exchange texts with S on my mobile, relaying the information that we are sailing soon and a fireworks display will send us off down Southampton Water behind the *Queen Elizabeth 2* which is leaving just ahead of us. The ship starts moving at 6pm, imperceptibly enlarging the gap between shipside and dockside. This is the start of a three month voyage that will take the *QM2* to Australia and back via Japan, China and the Gulf. She will return to Southampton only at the end of April. Now it is quite dark, surrounded by dock and far-off city lights. I can see we have cast off and are moving backwards. It is the start of my voyage of 6,000 miles to Cape Town.

Dinner in the Britannia restaurant starts at 6pm and I see it is already 6.15. I decide I want dinner even though I am late. When I get to my cabin to fetch my jacket, Dong is there preparing the room for the night and removing my empty wine bottle. I find the restaurant to the rear of Deck 2 and present myself to the *maître d'hotel*. A steward ushers me to table 55, set against wood panelling towards the centre of the restaurant. This is where I will dine each evening, with the same companions. The five other diners are there already so I feel late and apologise. Then, in the confusion of meeting five strangers at once, my mobile phone rings and I see it is S calling.

I can't immediately answer so let the introductions go on round the table. A menu is brought (they had been waiting for me before ordering). I nevertheless feel I must answer S so I get up and go into the lobby and call her.

It is to say goodbye. I sign off and rush back to the table. You only get one chance to make a first impression and mine seems to be going wrong. I order the first things I see on the lengthy menu – a breaded chicken roll starter with mayonnaise and pasta to follow.

After my initial confusion I find the company to be very agreeable. They are quite cordial in spite of my holding them up. Dinner aboard ship is all about conversation at table. To my right is Leo and next to him Joe. The lady opposite is obscured by the flower in the centre of the round table so I don't get to speak to her, but I later learn her name is Margaret, a widow travelling alone. To my left is a couple, Roger and his wife Carol, next to me.

They do not order drinks with their meal but I ask for a glass of champagne. It costs $17 with the service charge (about £10.80). All charges on board are in US dollars and you pay by presenting your card. At the end of the voyage the bill is charged to the credit card registered at check-in. Leo and Joe are travelling together and to my delight turn out to be Canadians. Leo is from Newfoundland and can talk mining as that is now one of the mainstays of the Newfoundland and Labrador economy. Joe is from Calgary which prompts a gush of information from me about the presence of my son and family there. He looks quite taken aback. It also results in my not finding out more about what he does in Calgary.

We chat about contrasts in politics and the economy between Canada and the UK. On the other side, with Roger and his wife Carol, we talk more about the ship and the voyage. Joe and Leo came across the Atlantic from New York to join the *QM2*. Leo is visiting Cape Town before flying back to Canada, while Joe goes on to Australia. Roger and Carol are going to Fremantle in Western Australia which takes four or five weeks.

Dinner enjoyed, I go back to the top deck and look forward over the prow. The ship is heading out through the Solent with the lights of the Isle of Wight on the starboard side and the lights of mainland Britain on the port side. There seem to be more lights straight ahead. I contemplate going somewhere for a drink but decide against it. It has been a long day and having been so busy at home in the weeks before leaving I think it is time to relax. So I go to my cabin to turn in.

I take my first shower. The bathroom is so clean it looks new; I remember the ship has had a complete refit since I was last on board. The shower spray is good though not exactly powerful. The water seems soft like we have at home from our water softener system. No doubt Cunard don't want the pipes scaling up with hard water. Later I find out the water supply is desalinated seawater which accounts for its softness. I go to bed early and do not sleep particularly well.

Wednesday 11 January

At Sea. Noon position 47N 7W

In bed I notice we are definitely afloat and the sea is the real master of this manmade behemoth. The carpet beneath my feet is alive with a gentle motion, so we must be on the Bay of Biscay. I imagine the waves come across the full reach of the North Atlantic driven by the prevailing westerly winds, with the water fetching up in the cup shape of the bay on the coast of Brittany, causing a cauldron in this confined space.

Life on board is regulated by the delivery of information sheets which are left in the cabin each evening when the steward turns down the bed. There is a news digest and a separate programme for the next day. Today's situation report from the navigator, published in the *Daily Programme*, says: "In the early hours of this morning we rounded the north-west tip of France, and entered into the Bay of Biscay. We shall continue our crossing of the bay for the rest of today, on a south-westerly heading, bound for Madeira." As I read, the ship heaves and gives a pronounced roll. Things on my desk shift and click together. The scale of the motion is still quite mild though.

The day's programme offers a mindboggling choice of activities. Typically, you might start your day with a fitness session or Catholic Mass, go on to social bridge or whist, then attend an iStudy workshop to brush up on your PowerPoint or Photoshop skills, learn napkin folding or watercolour painting, attend a fruit and vegetable carving demonstration, watch British Premiership football via a live satellite feed in the pub, watch an afternoon movie or listen to a classical piano recital, go to dancing class, attend a lecture on international relations, take part in a Texas hold 'em tournament in the Casino, or listen to a string quartet while you have afternoon tea.

In the evening, there's a harpist in the Chartroom bar, a string quartet in the Commodore Club, ballroom and Latin dancing, another movie, a variety stage show, a jazz club performance, a trivia quiz, and from 12.30am DJ Lee "plays the hits that keep you dancing all night long". The King's Court buffet is open until 4.30am for late night snacks, at which time it seamlessly opens for Continental breakfast. Food is free and no rationing, but you pay for alcoholic drinks.

It is now 6.30am and I feel hungry after my meatless day yesterday. I go to breakfast in the King's Court and line up to serve myself some coffee. I have a small plate of fruit, followed by a trip to the buffet. I choose an omelette and sausages, which the chef serves for me. They have a choice of American bacon (streaky crisp) and English (back). I choose American for a change. A few fried mushrooms provide a nod to the vegetable section, which has beans, tomatoes, and a rice hash.

After finishing, I strike up a conversation with the man at the next table who is also on his own. I think he is the chap who took a hit from the seagull yesterday but I am not sure. It does prove to be him. He says the steward took his coat away to be cleaned. When he told his friends back home what had happened (this was before we sailed) they all said it was a sign of good luck. Maybe it was a way to cheer him up, but it does not sound like good luck to me. Anyway this fellow, who seems quite shy and a good sort, is going to Fremantle travelling solo. We agree it will be nice to have some warm to hot sunny weather for a change after the last few disappointing summers in England.

We part and I go to my cabin to complete my ablutions. Of interest to me on the day's programme is a talk on Madeira, our first port of call, on Friday, and a get-together for solo travellers. On land this would be called a singles party. I decide against it because I'm not in search of company. I set off to explore the ship to remind myself where things are: the Queen's Ballroom for the Commodore's cocktails tonight and the pool which is situated on the same deck as my cabin. The ballroom extends the whole width of the ship at the waterline in the rear. I am disappointed the pool is not seawater as it was on Harold Nicolson's voyage in the *Willem Ruys* in 1957.

I go for a coffee on Deck 7 and sit outside watching the keen types marching round the perimeter of the ship on their walks – three times round is 1.1 miles. Most of them are elderly people with set expressions as if they are on serious and important business. It's as if this is part of their routine at home which must be continued at all costs on board. I feel like calling out "Don't forget you're on holiday!"

The talk on Madeira is in the Illuminations theatre that takes up two levels in the forward sections of Decks 2 and 3. It has starry lights in the ceiling and walls, and reclining seats. The lady giving the talk speaks with a broad South African accent and displays that self revealing naivety for which South Africans are famous (myself included). The talk gives tips on what to look out for when we visit Madeira. It is the only port of call for which I have booked myself a shore excursion.

We are told there is a famous hotel started by an Englishman in the late 19th century called Reid's, which is a tour excursion destination in itself. It seems to have the same vibes as Raffles in Singapore. Madeira has no beaches so it does not attract the young holidaymaker. Visitors are more interested in the lush gardens of the island, the clean mosaic decorated streets, old buildings, and markets. I reflect that the gardens and the walking would suit S and me for a holiday in a warm place that does not get too hot.

After the introduction to Madeira I go forward to Deck 8 to visit the Library and bookshop. I find a book on the history of the English gentry ("not part of the aristocracy nor of the mass of people below, but fed by both") written by Adam Nicolson, grandson of Harold. I decide against taking on such a tome as I have the *Dining with Churchill* book my daughter Lucy gave me for Christmas.

The adjoining bookstore is enlivened by another South African woman. She is behind the counter and getting matey in that disarming South African way with all the customers. She says to one, "This map is very good, you can mark the route you want to take then rub it off and mark another one, and if it rains the map will be all right". Everybody is her friend. She told someone else she is looking forward to getting off in Cape Town.

This is the second South African staff/crew member I've heard say that and later I hear others. It seems the South Africans are now ubiquitous, increasingly going foreign to enable them to make the living to which they are accustomed and to stay in their beloved country. Back in my cabin Dong interrupts me to hand me a book of Health Spa discount coupons that I put away in the drawer with the Gideon's Bible.

At eight bells (noon) the Commodore gives us a personal update of the progress of the voyage. We are 120 miles south west of Brest in the Bay of Biscay in 6,400ft of water and the temperature is 11C, or 52F. From Southampton we have covered 330 miles at a speed of 22 knots (25 miles per hour). The QM2 can comfortably exceed 30 knots, so she really is "cruising". By way of contrast, a fast 18th century East Indiaman did six or seven knots with a following wind while the 19th century clipper ship *Cutty Sark* could do 17 knots.

I put on my jacket for lunch and go down to the Chartroom bar and order a Martini. It costs $9 plus a 15 per cent service charge of $1.35 (about £6.50, not bad in my money). I sip it happily as the waves reel past in a flurry of white foam. The restaurant and adjacent cocktail bars are in the rear on Decks 2 and 3, so close to the waterline with a good view of the waves. The ship is very steady but you can always feel you are in motion, which is both obvious and reassuring.

Suitably fuelled, I go to the Britannia restaurant. There is no fixed seating plan for breakfast and lunch: you take pot luck who you are seated with; the whole point is to socialise. I am shown to a table by the window. There is a couple from Perth, Australia who are on a trip to celebrate his 50th birthday. He is a coffee merchant and we discuss the booming Western Australian economy based on mining. He agrees with me that the Government is running the risk of killing the economic miracle of the Lucky Country by imposing unrealistic taxation such as the carbon tax, which may be the highest in the world, and the new mining royalties.

The couple on my left are elderly and come from Cheam, a London suburb. He walks with difficulty and has to leave the table twice. His wife, a faded beauty with the exaggerated politeness of her generation, says he has drunk too much water. At the head of the table are a German couple who speak perfect English. He does most of the talking and is very knowledgeable about everything to do with ships and cruising. His wife is a champion bridge player. I ask what they call bridge in German as it is an English card game. He says they call it "bridge" as we do, and he adds that it was imported to Germany by British officers stationed in Hamburg at the end of the Second World War. The bridge champion has to leave for a scheduled game before our main courses are served. As a result the steward looks very crestfallen when he brings her food and she is not there.

I have a Greek salad starter and a mixed grill that is delicious and not too big. The food is very good but not, I think over the course of the voyage, as consistently good as in 2006. We discuss the dominance of German manufacturing. I point out that I drive a German car, travel to London in a German train and my kitchen is filled with German appliances. But apparently, like Britain, Germany is starting to outsource some of its manufacturing. Siemens kitchen appliances, for instance, are made in eastern European countries and are exactly the same machines as Bosch and AEG; they just have different brand badges.

The Australians leave first; he did not have a main course or pudding because he is watching his weight – not that he appears to need to. I go for a walk round Deck 7 and back to my cabin to read. I start *Dining with Churchill*, and take a nap. I don't want to mess up the bed so I move the duvet back and curl up on the end. I wake up at 4.45pm and have to be ready for the Commodore's cocktail party at 5.15pm. I take a shower and put on my new dress shirt with the cufflinks already inserted in the sleeves so that I would not forget them.

I have a major struggle fastening my bow tie. There is an adjustable silk strap that has to be hooked behind the bow and it is hard to see. This is going to be an ongoing challenge as I don't have S to help me and would rather not call for Dong when I am standing there with no trousers. To my relief I finally get it on and am ready to go in good time. I put the camera up on the shelf above the bed and set the timer for a picture of me in "full fig" for my first evening, which works out quite well.

At the entrance to the Queen's Ballroom I queue with some people I talked to in the terminal at Southampton. One of them is a retired army major and quite rude about South Africans in an affectionate joshing way. I get my picture taken with the Commodore, Christopher Rynd, and join the fray on the ballroom floor. I pick up a glass of wine and looking around catch the first person I see on his own to start a conversation. He doesn't seem much interested because he is looking for his wife, but she joins us and we talk. They are from south Devon so I say I know South Hams as we once spent Christmas at Greenway, a National Trust house that used to be Agatha Christie's home. Neither of them have heard of it, nor of Dittisham, the village over the Dart River from Greenway. It seems south Devon is a big place or perhaps they have limited horizons.

The Commodore gives a welcoming talk. He says of the 2,491 passengers on board, there are about 1,650 British, the most numerous group, followed by 247 Americans, 141 South Africans, and 131 Germans, plus many Canadians, Australians, Irish and Dutch. The Commodore's remarks are repeated by translators in French and German. The ship's complement of about 1,200 crew and hotel staff give a ratio of one person to every two passengers.

It is already 6pm so we are invited to go to dinner so that they can prepare for the later diners to have their cocktails with the Commodore. I am first at table 55 but am soon joined by Joe from Alberta on my right and Leo from Newfoundland on my left. I initially mix them up calling them by the wrong names but they are too polite to correct me at once. Joe says after my chat with Leo last night he learned things about Canada and the mining industry he did not know. Joe is in a dog collar and turns out to be a Catholic priest and semi-retired military chaplain, once based at Cold Lake, Alberta. We chat about young couples and the difficulties they have in making commitments. He does a bit of counselling so knows the score.

I talk to Leo about the ship. When the *QM2* was launched in 2004 at Saint-Nazaire in France she was, like her forebear the *Titanic* in 1912, the largest and most luxurious passenger liner afloat. She still keeps the luxury title but has been surpassed in size by *Oasis of the Seas* launched in 2009. At 1,132ft *QM2* is 250ft longer than the *Titanic*, while *Oasis* is only 49ft longer than *QM2*.

We discuss the ship's propulsion system. In my days as an Engine Room Mechanic in the South African Navy when I did national service in 1963, propulsion was achieved with steam driven reciprocating engines. Fuel oil was sprayed in a fine mist to burn in a chamber that heated water to raise steam for the engine. These engines gave way to turbines. The latest propulsion, used on the *QM2*, consists of electric engines fixed directly on the hull like the engines on the wings of aircraft.

Electricity drives propellers arranged in four pods at the stern and two on each side at the front. These make propeller shafts redundant, freeing up space in the stern. Two of the engine pods swivel so there is no need for a rudder. Changing the direction in which the propeller pod is pointing changes the direction of the ship.

In the industry I know, mine haul trucks use the same principle of direct drive. The trucks are as big as houses and as heavy as the Airbus A380. To eliminate the need for mechanical drive shafts to move such heavy loads, electric motive power is applied directly on the axles. Like *QM2*, on board diesel engines generate the electricity.

An interesting nugget from Leo is that while Carnival Cruise Lines of Miami own Cunard, they also own several well known brands including Holland America and P&O. Their business model is to let the cruise lines they own run themselves and the only two things on which Carnival have an overruling say is on the building of new ships and the purchase of fuel. Later in the voyage we will hear about a Carnival subsidiary called Costa Crociere, owner of the ill-fated *Costa Concordia* which I think puts a question mark over this hands-off business approach.

I am the only person to order wine. I have a delicious glass of red after having made rather a fool of myself when I thought I had ordered a white (I was having mozzarella tomato salad followed by Chinese duck) but got red. I called the steward over and he was quite right I was ordering from the red wine page of the wine list. Roger helps cover up my embarrassment with a kindly remark. The meal is good and we all get on well; there is lots to say.

At the table I notice Margaret fiddling with her mobile. She had been able to exchange texts but now there is no signal. I am reminded that Vodafone sent me a text after I had turned out the light on Tuesday, my first night, saying I was now on Vodafone Maritime and that outgoing calls cost 165 pence per minute and 130ppm to receive. Texts are 35 pence. I have a strong signal with all my bars showing. I experimented with a text to S and later received one back, slightly delayed because she had been at the movies. It is nice to know I have a means of keeping in touch.

After dinner most people were planning to attend a musical show featuring a vocalist called Jacqui Scott in the Royal Court theatre at 8.45pm. Instead I go to the Golden Lion pub for a live football game relayed by satellite from London featuring Tottenham Hotspur v Everton. The sound is loud and in stereo, so it is almost like being there. There are a number of gents who are hard core fans, some with longsuffering wives, other men who have come on their own. I order a Bass ale and stand to watch the game which is absorbing and very atmospheric.

It ends just in time for me to get to the Royal Court theatre to stand at the back and hear the last number. By way of prelude the singer says she played Evita in London. She sings *Don't cry for me Argentina* very well, with a powerful voice.

Next I go down to the Queen's ballroom where a grey haired mass of gents and ladies are tripping and twirling as if transported back to their youth. After a short while I carry on to the G32 nightclub situated right at the rear of the ship. It is named after the job number for the construction of the vessel. They have a much more upbeat band on the go singing numbers like *Kansas City Here I Come*, but there are few guests. I order a double whisky and listen to the music. Couples who are sitting nearby after half an hour take to the dance floor. Later, in the adjoining ballroom where the sound is more Glenn Miller they have a *Strictly Come Dancing* style exhibition of the cha-cha which is not what I remember the cha-cha to be like.

People start dispersing about 11.30pm so I call it a night. Feeling peckish, I stop off at the Deck 7 buffet and have a spoonful each of chilli con carne and Mexican rice which is just right to put me to sleep. After a struggle this time getting my tie off, I am into bed and soon asleep.

Thursday 12 January

At Sea. Noon position 39N 12W

I wake at 6.45am and get up to shave. Once I am shaved and dressed I feel better. I go down to Deck 7 to get tea. You queue up and the staff get quite cross if you try to serve yourself. I wanted a croissant but it had to be put on my plate by a waitress. It is something to do with hygiene and cleanliness which of course is all to the good. They have gel dispensers everywhere to sanitise your hands without washing with water. I tend to use them at inappropriate times like after I have eaten.

The seagull man is there again having his tea. We are evidently both early risers on the same routine. I greet him and tell him about the Spurs game (they won 2-0). He looks like a football lad but maybe he isn't. I drink my tea and go up to Deck 13, the sundeck, to look at the weather. The decks are wet from rain, the wind is cold and strong and the sky dark. Maybe when we get to Madeira tomorrow things will start to warm up.

The Navigator's update for today says: "Early this morning we rounded the north-west tip of Spain, at some 60 nautical miles, and continued on our south-westerly heading across the Iberian Abyssal Plain. We will continue on this heading until early tomorrow morning when passing the island of Porto Santo on our starboard side, and making our approaches to Madeira."

I go back to my cabin to change out of jeans and into chinos for breakfast in the Britannia Grill. I like to wear a jacket but perhaps later when it gets hot I will be more informal. I am shown to a large table of eight. On my right is a dull man who doesn't speak unless spoken to and does not let the conversation flow. It sounds like he has done a lot of cruising though he does not join activities. He speaks fondly of staying in his cabin with a book. At the other end of the table an Englishman is pouring an American woman a cup of tea. She's from Rochester, New York. He has large black rimmed spectacles. "How am I doing? How full is it? I can't see, I am almost blind after my stroke." Let it be said this is no loveboat and the majority of the passengers are very elderly, not that there is anything wrong with that. It makes me feel like a young buck again.

The lady on my left lives in Hawaii. She was born in England, moved with her family to Australia, met and married an American, lived in California and eight years ago moved to Hawaii. Her husband does not like to leave home much and likes to potter about in shorts and no shirt. She has been on a visit to the Isle of Wight and will disembark in Cape Town for a short holiday before flying back to Hawaii by way of New York and Los Angeles so she can make more visits.

I tell her I have also been a wanderer; moving from South Africa to Canada, and how tough it was settling down there and finding work, and then again adapting to Britain. But, I say, we've done well out of it, and here I am fortunate to be on a premier cruise liner on my way to Cape Town, which is where the whole exodus thing started. In an attempt at humour I say, "When I arrive in Cape Town they should have a welcome band playing on the dockside with banners proclaiming 'Home Boy Makes Good'".

I order two fried eggs on toast with English bacon, a sausage and a tomato. I notice the sky outside the window is brightening and there is a bit of colour; the sea looks increasingly blue. The lady from Hawaii ordered Eggs Benedict but the yolks are cooked hard yellow and she has left them. She does not complain, but orders a clean cup and fresh coffee. The ladies eat cereal. The couple with the dull man leave and then so do I, wishing everyone a good time.

On the way past the Purser's office I call in to ask about postage as I want to send postcards to my grandchildren with a picture of the ship. They have stamps and accept cards and letters for postage at Madeira so I know what to do. I also want to organise my disembarkation at Cape Town. My Cunard schedule says I get off on 25 January which is the second day of the ship's three-day stop in Cape Town. I can't very well remain on board for a whole day and night while my sister Val and her husband Stephen are on shore expecting my arrival.

After I had told the man from south Devon at the cocktail party my embarkation plans he had remarked that it might be better to disembark early before the bunfight that will ensue with hundreds of passengers leaving the ship on the 25th. The purser person says it is okay and they will give me a time of departure on the 24th.

I return to my cabin. The stewards are changing all the mattresses in the staterooms, putting in new ones which they haul out of a service alley and strip off the plastic protective wrapping. Dong says I get a new mattress too. I change back into jeans and go on a tour of the decks. The sun is out and the wind not that cold. The noon report from the Commodore puts us 896 miles from Southampton going at a speed of 23 knots over an ocean depth of 14,000ft. On Deck 7 on the sunny port side many people wrapped in their sweaters, hats and scarves are lying on the loungers with eyes closed, face to the sun. Their appearance confirms a statistic I came across that the average age of passengers on the ship is 70 years.

I find there is a small observation area near my cabin on Deck 12 where you can view the bridge and the officers conning the ship. They have banks of radar screens and closed circuit television images. The ship's wheel is the same diameter as a dinner plate: it looks smaller than a car steering wheel. There are instructions on how to take it off autopilot and use it manually.

In Nelson's navy the ships had a double steering wheel – two wheels back to back with their handles sticking out of the circumference. It took 16 men to haul them to and fro to keep the ship on course by means of chains attached to the rudder. It was just muscle against the pull of the sea and the currents. Now there is no helmsman, and no rudder for that matter. The officer in charge, a young man, sits in the teenage slouch position in the raised conning chair, chatting to another officer. It doesn't look as if there is much to do on a quiet day.

But there have been unquiet days. A letter posted on the wall in the viewing area with other memorabilia recounts a sea rescue of a small craft by the *QM2* in a storm off Nova Scotia in October 2010. The letter from the Canadian Coast Guard at Dartmouth NS says the *QM2*'s officers displayed the highest standards of maritime prowess to save lives in gales and rough seas notwithstanding the size of the liner compared to the craft that was rescued. It is reassuring to know that in an emergency the boys on the bridge can indeed spring into action and save the day.

I go to lunch at the King's Court buffet and queue in a small line-up. I have garden vegetables, baked chicken and mash with gravy, which tastes delicious. Then back to another food bar for a bowl of cubed melon. The food makes me sleepy so I am off to my cabin for a rest until it is time for the afternoon movie.

Chariots of Fire is being screened in the Illuminations theatre at 3pm. The two theatres – the other is the Royal Court – are in the forward section of the ship and the Britannia restaurant and Queen's Ballroom are aft, but I have been mixing them up and going aft for the theatre. No matter, lots of time. I thought I had seen the movie before, but it is all new to me. *Chariots of Fire* was made in 1981 so it is celebrating its 31st anniversary in this year of the London Olympics with the release of a digitally remastered version and a stage play.

The director, Hugh Hudson, is there to talk about the film before they screen it. He says it was his first feature movie after several years making documentaries and TV ads, such as those quirky British Airways ads with the faces. He is proud that *Chariots of Fire* won an Oscar. He has since made several films, the latest being *Rupture* which has not yet had its premiere. The latest film was inspired by his actress wife Maryam d'Abo after she had a brain aneurism in Los Angeles. He says she came to within an inch of her life. He made the film to portray the burden which illness brings not only to the sick but to those like family who provide support. The film is to be screened later in the voyage before we get to Cape Town.

Chariots of Fire tells the story of a group of brilliant athletes at Cambridge University in the early 1920s preparing for the 1924 Olympic Games in Paris, "with hope in their hearts and wings on their heels". The movie starts with a wonderful sequence where the hero, Harold Abrahams (this is a true story) races round the quad at Gonville and Caius College within the time it takes for the clock to strike the hour of noon.

The whole movie is so true to the period in terms of dress and cars and settings I see it as the prototype of films like *Brideshead Revisited*, *Upstairs Downstairs* and the more recent *Downton Abbey*. The music, with the iconic theme tune played while the runners are training on a beach in the opening sequence, is totally integrated with the pictures and there are some charming scenes that incorporate snatches of Gilbert & Sullivan with those catchy tunes like *Three little girls are we* from the *Mikado*. Abrahams, after a lot of setbacks, triumphs in Paris by winning the Men's 100 yard dash, beating the Americans against the odds. In real life, he went on to be a top athletics administrator after marrying his sweetheart, Sybil, whom he first saw in a production of the *Mikado*.

Hudson says *Chariots of Fire* is being revived as part of the cultural festival surrounding the 2012 London Olympics, and I can see why – a proud depiction of British grit and raw talent winning the day. I am quite smitten and glad I went to see it. The movie and Q&A with the director ends at about 5.20pm and I go back to my cabin to change for formal dinner. I am a bit quicker with the bow tie this time.

I have a swift gin and bitter lemon in the Golden Lion pub and chat to an elderly gent at the bar. The others are already seated when I get to the table and I find myself beside Margaret who I have not spoken with before. One by one we order our two courses, the steward writing it down on a pad. The steward is very attentive and expert at creating the feel-good factor. Some of us wonder about his/her gender – not that it matters, we're just curious. The figure is male, with trousers, and the hair is slicked back in a sleek sheen with a male-like parting, similar to the dinner jacketed Julie Andrews in *Victor Victoria*. But the face, voice, hands and fingernails look feminine. Other female stewards wear skirts. I thought our steward was called Alice but it turns out to be Alex, which could be male or female so we are none the wiser.

I order Spanish Serrano ham and the rack of lamb. The ham is very sparse and comes on a bun to stretch it out. The lamb is delicious and cooked just right – pink. The others complain of the pinkness and I explain that chefs disdain well done meat because it loses its flavour. I repeat a story from my son Guy, who is executive chef at a Calgary golf club, that when there is an order for well done meat the chef reaches into the back of the freezer because the diner is not going to taste it anyway.

In conversation with Margaret she tells me that she has been a widow for two years following the death of her husband from mouth cancer, which she attributes to smoking and drinking. He worked in the Portsmouth dockyards. He had a lesion on his tongue that was taken out but then the cancer appeared in his gums, after which his teeth were taken out to try and stop the spread.

But, she says, the cancer reappeared in his jaw because it was transmitted through the stems of his tooth implants. While he was undergoing treatment she had a health check which led to a scan that revealed cancer in her own kidney. So she found herself in the horrific situation of having chemotherapy for her own cancer while her husband was fighting for his life. She survived and he did not. She says the whole experience has been a nightmare and has blighted her life forever. However she has a "partner" now who lives in France and he is "sorting himself out as to what he wants to do" while she is away on a three month world voyage. "A shroud has no pockets", she says, meaning you can't take your money with you to the grave. I admire her fortitude and cheerfulness in the face of such setbacks.

I learn Leo was a teacher in Newfoundland. He says his dream job would have been to be a librarian on a cruise ship. He met such a person once who looked after a large library on a China registered ship that served as a floating branch of a university. During summer holidays when university was closed the ship was used for Alaska cruises out of Vancouver in the early days of cruising. He thinks looking after a floating library summer and winter is the best job he can think of. He remarks the *QM2*'s library, billed as the largest afloat, is not a patch on this other one. It seems Leo's fulltime retirement occupation is cruising, and he is very knowledgeable.

After dinner I look in on a second showing of *Chariots of Fire* in the Illuminations theatre. I've missed the beginning which I wanted to see again so I don't stay long. I decide to have an early night. There is a dance revue that does not appeal and I don't feel like a drink. I go to my cabin and read, then take a shower, organise a laundry bag for Dong to take tomorrow and go to bed. I sleep extremely well, better than I can remember for months.

Friday 13 January

Funchal, Madeira

We are due into Funchal at 8.30am but dock before 8am. I miss the arrival because I went to breakfast at the appointed time of 7.30am, thinking I would be out by 8.30am. Earlier, I woke to my alarm at 6am and got ready before going up to my lookout point to see the weather and discover what is going on. There is a lookout deck one level above the bridge facing forward with glass panes. There is never anyone else there so I have it to myself. I see the lights of the island of Porto Santo on the starboard bow. The island of Madeira is behind it, a short way south. Madeira means "wooded" which is the way it was when the Portuguese discovered it in the 15th century when the first navigators were pushing the envelope southwards. They found Porto Santo first then Madeira later, which was much more of a find as it was much larger.

I go down to Deck 7 to get a coffee and a croissant. I meet my morning friend and discover his name is Dennis. We get on well and have a nice friendly chat. He is going ashore independently for a walkabout.

At breakfast I have my back to the window and the view of sunny Madeira. I am seated next to a widow on my left and a couple from Lincolnshire on my right. They are dressed to play golf and are going ashore for a game. When they get to Cape Town they will spend a six-week holiday playing golf. They play regularly in South Africa as they think the courses are top-notch. They take a cottage on the Cape coast at Hermanus, and love it there.

A man opposite asks me where I lived in Canada and he tells me he spent 17 years in Montreal. He is a distiller and worked for Seagrams. He says he had to learn French double quick because in Quebec they don't do English. But he thinks the French Canadians the most charming, friendly people and Montreal an unusual city, especially for North America.

The widow next to me recognises my sympathetic ear and pours out such a tale of woe and successive disasters that she makes me feel quite depressed. She is British but emigrated to Australia. Her husband died six months ago and she almost starts weeping. Her children are unhelpful and the relatives she visits dutifully in England at great expense are rude and dismissive. Oh yes, and she tripped over a chair on Deck 7 and has had to spend $200 on treatment for a twisted back and sore neck.

She and her husband bought their dream house a week before he died and she has since moved twice. Her son was buying a property – this is in Western Australia where she lives south of Perth – and asked her to come and live nearby. So she moved there and then his deal fell through and now she is stranded in a place she doesn't want to be. As I leave the table I ask her to take care and I really mean it.

I go on deck and take pictures of Funchal, the houses in terraces up the hillside, all looking neat in cream with red roofs in the sunshine. I see a gondola going up the mountain. At the dock are buses and swarms of taxis. I have booked a shore excursion for $53 for three hours which starts at 10am. I have to join the group at the Royal Court theatre at 9.40am. I now discover that most people avoid the shore excursions because they are expensive compared to going it alone. But it is convenient and it strikes me that I don't have local currency to take a taxi.

I meet my "Scenes of Madeira" tour party in the Royal Court. A steward is selling bottles of water at $2.75

a pop; Cunard don't miss a trick. An usher holding a No 13 paddle aloft leads us to the gangway on Deck 2. We queue to show our passenger cards, then cross the gangway to land and board a comfortable modern coach with a stately flower of Madeira painted on the side. I sit beside a man who left his wife aboard and came on the tour alone. The tour guide is a mature man called John who speaks perfect English. Later I hear he had a Scottish father and lived for a while in England. But now, judging from his descriptions he is very proud to be Madeiran.

We go into town from the breakwater, about 3km, and find it to be very attractive, clean and full of flowers, gardens and greenery. On the way to our first attraction, the Pico dos Barcelos, a peak with a viewpoint, John tells us such things as Madeira is not a small island, it is 500 square miles (about three times the Isle of Wight). He points out the tropical greenery and says farming is economically more important to Madeira than tourism. The island farmers grow grapes for Madeira wine, bananas by the ton, avocados, mangoes and paw-paw. The route through the suburbs is a blaze of colour, featuring poinsettia, bougainvillaea, hibiscus, jasmine and the famous flame trees found in Africa.

At the Pico there is a restaurant. The menu on the window advertises *espada* served with bananas. A number of people have mentioned to me that this is a delicious fish you can get only in Madeira. It lives at a great depth and dies when brought to the surface because of the change in air pressure. We look at the view around us, of the patterns of houses strewn over the steep landscapes along the ridges like a scattering of white pebbles. We take pictures, including the *QM2* far below in the haze. I get a man in a Springbok rugby jersey to take my picture. He flew from Johannesburg to London to take the *QM2* back to South Africa.

A South African couple I met on the first night on deck in Southampton are there. They came on the hop-on, hop-off bus. They are so open and friendly and their hearts are in the right place. We reboard the bus. Getting in and out is a drawn out process because most of the passengers are very slow on their feet and need help up or down the steps. Next we head for a fishing village called Camara de Lobos, where Winston Churchill is said to have come to paint in the 1950s. There is a Churchill bar in the village but it has gone bust and is closed. The village is attractive and enclosed with a tiny beach at the end of the cove for landing fish. The bus climbs out of the village and heads upward along steep, winding roads.

Madeira's inhabitants live in houses clinging to precipitous slopes, a marvel of geotechnical engineering. Each house has a flat patch of ground made possible by dry stone wall terracing, using the local volcanic basalt rock. It must have taken centuries to accomplish by hand. They grow all kinds of vegetables, from cabbages to onions and all the rest. I've always known the Portuguese since the days of the fresh produce shops in Johannesburg as a nation of market gardeners and it must have started here.

Apparently these productive terraces on what was once sheer barren mountainside have been designated a World

Heritage site. A minor crop today is sugar cane which was once a gold mine for Madeira in the old days when sugar was a scarce luxury. Sugar cane was sent to Brazil, a Portuguese colony, where it thrived and eventually became so prolific that it undercut Madeira in price and ruined their industry.

On the way back from Cabo Girao, a 2,000ft clifftop said to be the second highest in Europe, John stops the bus to let us take photos of the wondrous terraces. He tells us they are irrigated by *lavadas*, canal streams that follow the contours of the slopes to bring water from the top of the peaks. I ask where the water comes from. He says it is simply there, percolating down to aquifers replenished by rain. A bit worryingly, he adds that it has not rained properly over Madeira since last October. If you buy land in Madeira you automatically get water rights. You can open the sluice on the *lavada* and take your water, but not continuously. Each farmer has a designated irrigation time with a set duration. My ears prick up when I hear there are numerous trails for walkers that follow the contours of the *lavada*s. That would make a pleasant holiday activity.

We end our tour at a Madeira wine salesroom in downtown Funchal. We are given a generous glass to taste. It is fortified wine like sherry but has a good depth of flavour. It goes well with cheese or dessert, or just as an aperitif. I pay £8 on my debit card for a bottle of five-year-old medium dry.

We board the bus and go back to the mole where the mighty ship is moored. To my surprise I see the familiar red maple leaf flag flying on a warship alongside the same dock. It is a Canadian navy frigate. I walk back from where the bus drops us alongside the *QM2* to have a closer look. Even more of a coincidence is that this is HMCS *Vancouver*. The security gate on the dockside is open and I approach a woman crew member who is there. I greet her and announce I'm a Canadian citizen and come from Vancouver even though I don't sound like it. I ask if I can take a picture. She says sure, but from outside the gate.

Chatting to her, she says the ship has been on station in the Mediterranean as part of the NATO force protecting people in Libya. Now they are on their way home. The stopover in Madeira is for three days. The *Vancouver* is based in Victoria, British Columbia, so they go back through the Panama canal. Later when I am back on board the *QM2* I see they have moved closer to us on the dockside to make room for another ship and are just beneath the *QM2*'s stern that towers over the small grey frigate. I hear the bosun's whistle calling and an announcement being made in Canadian tones as seamen gather on the deck in their baseball cap headgear and blue grey uniforms.

At about 2.30pm I have a good meal at the King's Court buffet. They have ragout of lamb and Singapore rice, both of which are spicy. The lamb is melt-in-the mouth tender, braised I suppose, just the way I like it. Now we have been on board for more than two days, the catering staff have given up serving us and we serve ourselves. Dennis, my mate from the mornings, told me today that this is normal practice as by now if someone had brought a virus on board we would know about it.

I take a turn round the deck. There are lots of people sunning themselves now: the weather is the warmest since England and full of promise. I stay in my cabin until 4pm and then go upstairs to view our departure for Tenerife, our next port of call, a night's sail to the south and on the latitude of the Sahara desert.

I buy a beer at the bar on the pool deck just down from my cabin on Deck 12 and take it outside to the sundeck. I use one of the loungers with the backrest as upright as possible so that I can admire the view of Madeira and sip my beer, which is cold and delicious. The sun is out but there is a cool breeze and I need my baseball cap and green wind-breaker jacket. Later there is a band called VIBZ, the one from the G32 nightclub, playing popular tunes on the stern deck to see us off from Madeira. They call it Sailaway music.

I stand at the railing on Deck 13 to look down on the deck terraces at the stern. People are starting to look very informal now the weather is warming up. The music lifts my spirits and makes me enjoy even more the wonderful situation I find myself in. I watch the hump of Madeira receding in the dusk behind us as the ship heads south, leaving a broad wake of aquamarine water that has the peculiar effect of flattening the surface of the sea like a roadway through the waves.

My mobile phone has had no signal all day though I had one while at sea after leaving British phone-space. Once we are away from Madeira I get my Maritime Communications Network signal back with full signal bars even when the phone is in my cabin safe enclosed by metal. It must be because my cabin is so close to that big white globe on the sundeck marked MCN, the satellite aerial. I text S to arrange to call in the morning.

At dinner we all ask each other what we did that day. The Canadians seem to know all about the Canadian frigate and don't appear as impressed as I was. The acoustics seem bad this evening and I can't hear what Joe is saying so it is a bit awkward. We discuss all the ways that Cunard squeezes passengers for money by increasing the prices of amenities like the Funchal cablecar compared to going it alone. I tell them I thought my excursion well worth it as the guide was interesting and we saw a broad overview of the city and surroundings. I have salmon terrine to start followed by pork escalope, which is delicious. Bread and butter pudding that comes like a hockey puck is not a great choice.

I always have a glass of wine with my meal so the steward knows to come over. Nobody else will touch a drink, maybe to economise, so I no longer ask if anyone will join me or whether we should order a bottle. I suspect they are deterred by the principle of Cunard adding an automatic service charge to every order. A pint of Bass at the pool bar costs $5.25 and 79 US cents are added for a total of $6.04. Tonight's white Sauvignon blanc house wine at table is $9.95 and with the service charge comes to $11.44. These seem reasonable to me, especially as this is a super special holiday.

Margaret says she takes a one litre empty plastic water bottle to breakfast, orders orange juice and fills the bottle which, diluted with water, keeps her in drinks all day for free. I ask how she manages to pour under the table but she just laughs: to such lengths do they go to avoid the Cunard service charge. To replace a 1.5 litre Cunard Natural Mineral Water bottle in the minibar of the cabin costs $3.95. It doesn't affect me as I drink tap water which I find agreeable, and I don't use the soft drink mixers in the minibar either ($2.50 a can). My minibar is untouched for the whole voyage.

Dong puts out a bucket of ice on the table every day as part of doing up the room. I don't use it, but I sometimes hear strange sounds in the dark and I've come to realise they come from the ice cubes melting and settling in the container. Talking to a chap on deck once, who was killing time before dinner while his wife got ready, he said they spend a lot of time in their cabin with the sea view from the balcony, watching TV and mixing their own drinks. You can buy duty free liquor at the shop on board and use it in your cabin. However I would be a sad person doing that on my own in an inside cabin, so I head for the bar.

Cunard says in its Voyage Guide that the service charge is shared among the staff: If true, I have no problem with that. I met a room service steward in the lift one morning on the way to breakfast. He was taking tea on a silver tray to someone in bed and I asked him conversationally how things were going. He said they were very busy and under stress with the ship full of demanding passengers. I reflect that the poor chap probably gets told off for taking so long as he pants into the cabin with the blessed tea. I have overheard passengers being unnecessarily rude to staff when something is not to their liking or a food item has run out. Like my son Guy in the hospitality industry, I always think people in roles that contribute to our enjoyment deserve recognition. On the other hand, fare paying passengers should not be expected to top up pay levels.

After dinner I go to Illuminations to see the 8pm movie, *Henry V*, a 1980s version of Shakespeare's play featuring Kenneth Branagh. It is heavy going and requires close concentration so I just want to get through it. I then go to bed to read my Churchill book at 10.15pm. In contrast to the film I have just seen, the book is a bit lightweight but of some interest. I expected it to be more about Churchill's power of conversation, rather than a compendium of official events with their menus. When I chose to take *Dinner with Churchill* with me on the voyage I thought, tongue in cheek, I might get some tips for dinner conversation, but I am disappointed.

I turn off the light and go into a deep relaxing sleep like last night. I am feeling great, with my cold and sniffles gone and no more coughing fits. I am sure the English winter is bad for my health.

Chapter 2

Bulge

Saturday 14 January

Santa Cruz de Tenerife, Canary Islands

$\mathcal{M}$y alarm rings at 6.15am and somehow I feel reluctant to get up. I ask myself why I set the alarm and remember I want to have an early breakfast and be ready to phone S as arranged last night. It suddenly occurs to me that, like Madeira, I might not have a signal when we enter port at Santa Cruz and she will wonder why I did not phone. My phone still has a full signal from MCN so I text her and explain I might not get through.

Once shaved I feel more alive. I go on my usual route to the Lookout on Deck 13 at the front of the ship and see the lights of Tenerife on the starboard bow. Harold Nicolson says in his book that the Spanish explorers found these islands full of wild dogs so called them the "Caninas" islands, *canina* being the word for dog. This was corrupted by British sailors into "Canaries" and the name stuck.

It is still dark but the wind is milder, the chilly edge of the north has gone. I cross the expanses of the sundeck and go down to Deck 7 for my tea. Dennis is in his usual spot, reading the *Daily Programme*. He did an independent trip around Madeira yesterday and I tell him about my successful tour. He asks me what there is to do in Durban (South Africa). All I can think of are the beaches and I tell him I don't know Durban very well.

This leads on to why I left South Africa and what I think about it now, and all that. I tell him I no longer feel a bond with the place as I have lived elsewhere for so long, although I can't help speaking like one of them. Having had my coffee and a croissant, I get up to serve myself breakfast and we part company. Breakfast is okay but not great. There are no warm plates so by the time you have put egg on a cold plate and waited for your toast to be made the food is nearly cold. I decide to get the toast first in future then go back to the end of the line for the hot food. After scrambled egg, bacon and sausage I have a plate of melon, and a banana, having seen so many banana trees in Madeira.

Suddenly, without warning, the ship is motionless and in port, tied up alongside a long concrete mole with a view of the jagged south-facing mountains of Santa Cruz. It is not yet light but the sharp peaks are silhouetted against the sky in grand fashion. A white neon sign in the shape of a Christian cross sits atop the most prominent peak.

The stark mountains look down on where in 1797 Britain's naval hero Admiral Horatio Nelson lost his right arm in a failed assault on Santa Cruz, his elbow shattered by grapeshot. The Royal Navy was trying to capture the harbour so they could ambush the Spanish treasure ships when they made landfall from South America. Now it is an outpost of peaceable but treasureless Euro-land.

My phone pings and I get a text message saying I am connected to the Spanish mobile phone network. The signal says the provider is Orange. The cost of a call is 75p a minute, half that of the Maritime service, so I can chat longer with S. Back in my room I receive a text from S saying she is in the house and ready for my call. The first attempt does not work because the way her number is set up on my contact list is wrong for international calls. A helpful text display gives the correct sequence and I press that and get through after a long pause.

The signal in my cabin is not great so I go up on deck to the Lookout where the reception is perfect. We have a good catch-up with me telling her how we must visit Madeira, all about *Chariots of Fire* and Hugh Hudson's new movie *Rupture*, and how much I am enjoying myself. Her news is about frosts and covering my potted fuchsia with fleece, how work is going on and her attendance of a compulsory course. Basically all is well and she is happy.

While we are talking the Commodore makes his announcement about visiting Santa Cruz, that the gangways are open to go ashore, the weather is good. He signs off with "Have a good time but be back by 4.30 pm". So with the phone line open S gets a flavour of shipboard life. We end our conversation and agree to exchange text messages from now on as there is no need for another voice call. It is ten days to Cape Town for me and two weeks for her until we are reunited.

I go back to the cabin and find I am locked out as I did not take my passenger card when I left the room to get a better phone signal on deck. I find Dong straight away, but he gets in first with his concern: I did not put my name and stateroom number on my laundry chit so the bag has been returned. This seems to be a major concern to him so I tell him not to worry. I do the necessary and it will now be two days before I get the clean laundry which I was expecting today. He lets me into my cabin.

Planning my day, I have no urge to go ashore, so will stay put and potter about, and maybe have a first swim. The daily schedule of events says there is a live football game at 2.30pm by satellite in the Golden Lion pub, Manchester United v Bolton Wanderers. I decide that will be the highlight of my day and I can happily sink a few beers.

At 10am the ship's company hold a shipboard incident response exercise involving a simulation of a fire breaking out in a passenger cabin on Deck 10. There are crew announcements over the loudspeakers but no action is required of us "guests". They have these exercises weekly so the crew are prepared if anything happens. Apparently these days the biggest fear in the maritime world is of fire, not sinking, nor hitting an iceberg.

I go on the top sundeck with my camera and binoculars and take in the sights of Santa Cruz de Tenerife. The mountains are much less attractive in the bright light of day; they are hard and parched, unclothed except for light green semi-arid shrubs dotted about. The distant aspects are enveloped in the heat haze mingled with Sahara dust that I remember from our holiday at Los Gigantes which is on the south side of the island. The city itself is a stark jumble of boxy apartment blocks and office buildings. I remember overhearing a chap say Santa Cruz is more of an industrial port than a resort city.

A tender is alongside delivering fuel to the *QM2* and crew members are lined up at the rail as their safety simulation carries on. There is a banner fastened to the outside of the railings on Deck 7 facing the land side and the basin of the dock. It says in English: "Security Warning Keep 50m Away". I hope waterborne citizens can read English so they don't come close enough to put limpet mines on the hull. *Why did the submarine blush? Because it saw Queen Mary's bottom.* An announcement tells the crew they can now stand down from their safety exercise.

I go back to my cabin and stow my camera and binoculars, and change into the swim shorts I bought for the trip. They fit well and I feel comfortable in them.

I put on sun screen and T-shirt and head for the pool barefoot and with my sun hat. The green striped loungers are set up in rows each side of the pool, each with a neatly rolled green swim towel in place.

I choose a spot that is not in direct sun and settle down. It is bliss just to sit there. Elderly folk are dog paddling about. It is 4ft 6in at the shallow end and 5ft 3in at the deep end. The pool is not very big, about 20ft long and 16ft wide. There is a raised lip of mosaic tiles that you have to climb over to get into the pool. I expect this is to stop the water sloshing out in bad weather. There are two hot tubs in raised positions at the shallower end.

An elderly lady helps herself up the stairs to the hot tub with the aid of a crutch. In addition to the rows of loungers on each side of the pool there are two table tennis tables in one corner of the space and a bar on the opposite side with a bandstand between them. The roof of the pool is open for the first time: it slides back like a sports stadium roof and the huge funnel of the ship, black and red, looms over us. It is all so perfect. I order a Bass from a steward called Edgardo and he brings it to me without me having to get up.

You have to sign a chit for each drink. Edgardo tells me they don't run tabs, each sale has to be "closed" individually. I then go for a swim and the water is lovely, not too hot and not too cold, just like Goldilocks' porridge. I have the pool to myself so I do a few strokes and swim from one end to the other underwater. I get out, dry off and return to my beer and staring into space. I have a second beer and decide I should go to the

Britannia restaurant for lunch. I go back to the cabin to change, happy in the convenience of staying on the same deck as the pool, just a short distance away.

In the restaurant I am seated with a British couple who regard themselves as Capetonians because they lived there for an extended period and go back frequently to see friends. We have an animated chat over an excellent lunch. I have steak and ale pie. I can feel the pressure building from the beer so I have to excuse myself when I have finished eating. I say by way of explanation I've had some beers round the pool and will be right back.

The British-Cape Town lady, who I've been telling that I feel more Canadian than South African, laughingly says as I get up: "You may not think you're a South African but with beers round the pool and wine with your lunch you're definitely South African!" I think it is meant as a compliment and I find it quite revealing about myself. Am I the only one who is indulging? "It is only because I am unsupervised at the moment," I reply to more laughter. I have trouble finding a toilet but am soon back for dessert.

I get to the Golden Lion early for the football game. The channel for the football is not on yet and one of the British fans is complaining. He tells the unfortunate barman, "If it doesn't get sorted in time there's going to be a damn good flogging". The young barman looks quite taken aback, repeating under his breath the scary word "flogging".

The game comes on and the beers are lined up on the bar, each glass in front of a football fan on a barstool, with rows of people behind sitting further back. The bar person lays out generous bowls of salty crisps to keep us thirsty. Manchester United beat Bolton 3-0 even though the Bolton goalkeeper makes some brilliant saves, including stopping a penalty kick. At half time I go up to Deck 7 for a snack and find they have hot dogs on offer (and hamburgers) with the proper buns. I have a hot dog with butter and the fixings and it is as good as in America. After the game I go back for another one, a move I later regret because I can hardly eat my dinner in the Britannia.

I go up on the sundeck for our departure from Tenerife. The VIBZ band is playing its Sailaway music on the stern deck among the Princess Grill passengers who pay top dollar and get the poop deck to themselves. We can watch from the overlooking Deck 13. It seems that others do indulge as there is a scrawny chap in a bathing suit gyrating to the music in a most amusing caricature of a rock star with lots of encouragement and laughter.

The ship is docked nose in to the harbour basin so it pushes away from the dock with its bow thrusters and backs out slow astern, the rear of the ship turning towards the open sea around the end of the breakwater. The sharp end then comes round to point south and the QM2 sets off leaving a white flecked churn of blue green water in its wake. The band packs up, inviting people to go to the G32 nightclub from 9.45pm and to bring their dancing shoes.

It is 5.50pm so time to put on my jacket and go to dinner. I am seated between Leo and Joe and unsurprisingly have no appetite. I choose the least filling food, an avocado and tomato salad which I can't finish and a grilled halibut. I leave most of the rice.

The conversation is about Tenerife which did not seem to impress anyone much. I chat with Joe, who turns out to be quartered with the crew as he is the ship's Catholic priest on board, so is working, at least part time. I have noticed an entry on the programme "Mass with Father Maclean", and this is he. He tells me his tour of duty ends in Fremantle (Perth) where he has a number of friends. Then he flies to Honolulu to see more friends before returning to Calgary. His timings are uncertain and he is worried his travel insurance might run out before he gets to Canada. He won't risk even one day without insurance. We talk about happiness and the need to be happy.

He was a military chaplain and tells me that a young man once came to see him with a problem: he was in love with a Caribbean girl and wanted to marry her but his parents absolutely forbade it. So, says Joe, "I asked him which of his parents did he find most easy to talk to. It was his father. I advised him to take his father aside and ask 'Do you want me to be happy?'

"Of course the father is likely to say 'yes'. Then the young man could say, either I make you happy by not marrying my girl, or by marrying her I make myself happy. If I choose to make only you happy my resulting unhappiness may lead to breakdown and all manner of evils. Is that really what you want?" This brought the

Dad round, the son married his sweetheart and the parents became reconciled to the idea. I comment it was good advice. It is no good standing in the way of your child's happiness whatever your own views and feelings. They must do for themselves, not for the parents who they will outlive anyway.

I ask Leo what he is reading. He says a Berlitz annual guidebook *Cruises and Cruising* about the industry, the sort of book you flip through and look up things. It's about all the cruise ships, their technology and markets, what's coming up new and so on. He borrowed it from the *QM2* library and he says there is a waiting list for it so he had better hurry. Copies are on sale in the bookshop. I later check it out and it costs £17 but does not interest me.

We get up to leave the dining room. I decide I have had enough for the day. I need to regroup in the cabin. My laundry has come back sooner than expected. The shirts are immaculately laundered. My socks, underpants and hanky are all neatly folded in a paper bag.

I check my mobile for any traffic. My phone indicates two missed calls, one from S, the other number I do not recognise. I phone S and get her, but it is quite redundant as she did not call me at all. I suspect it is an old call which is catching me up. Anyway I have a quick exchange with S and she reminds me she is going down to Bristol to see great granny tomorrow. I go to bed, read a bit of *Dinner with Churchill*, and turn out the light. I sleep well again.

Sunday 15 January

At Sea. Noon position 22N 17W

I am awake at 6am without the alarm, and get up as I am soon bored with being in bed. I shower and shave and put on my shorts for the first time. I go up to the Lookout. It is still too dark to see anything (this is nearly 7am) but there is a white steady light far off astern on the port side. We are near the furthest extent of the bulge of Africa. The wind has a warm touch. I go down to Deck 7 and see Dennis who is just leaving. He tells me he was awake at 5am. He sees my shorts and looking down at his usual track pants says maybe he should change.

At the buffet there are very few people. A woman with grey hair still dishevelled from bed and wearing the white standard issue Cunard towelling dressing gown is there to have coffee. A head steward tells her she is in breach of the dress code but she can take some coffee, which she does. But she doesn't go away, she sits down at a table. It is not a pretty sight; but maybe she's just home-sick for a sit-down in her kitchen.

The navigator's report reads: "On the first sea day from Tenerife to Walvis Bay [a distance of 3,800 miles] *Queen Mary 2* will steer a south, south-easterly course until she reaches a point some 50 miles due west of Cap Blanc otherwise known as Ras Nouadhibou, which is a 40 mile peninsula on the African coast by the Tropic of Cancer."

My plan for today is to go to a Cunard Insights lecture on international relations at 10am, a Hugh Hudson movie at

1pm, another Insights lecture at 3.30pm on the loss of the Russian navy submarine *Kursk*, and second movie after dinner at 8pm called *Super 8*. It's Sunday, and the schedule says Father Maclean is holding Catholic Mass at 8.30am. There is an inter-denominational service conducted by the Commodore in the Royal Court theatre at 11am at which there will be a collection of money for seafarers' charities.

Somebody else's laundry is delivered to my cabin. The chit has my name on it. Curiously it is a copy of the chit in my handwriting for my previous laundry but the date is different as well as the cost. I leave it out with a note to Dong saying there is a mix-up. Dong now calls me Mr Charles (my official passenger name is Charles Leggatt to match my passport).

The lecture on the 21st century international order is by a former US Ambassador, Howard Walker. He discusses the relative decline of Western Europe and how the traditional North Atlantic community is losing clout to the emergence of the Asia Pacific. He thinks the US will continue to be powerful but it will no longer be the only superpower. Europe may have had peace for 70 years, a remarkable achievement, but there is still disunity over the monetary union. He says loans to EU entrants are used to make lifestyle improvements such as good public sector jobs and generous health and social services, but not enough is put to productive investment that will keep Europe competitive.

The Eurozone can only work on the assumption that all the countries have similar economic strengths, but there is a gulf in attitudes between northern Europe (mainly Germany) and the Mediterranean countries. In Germany the word for debt has connotations of guilt; Germans are terrified of being in debt. They live to work, that is their reason for being (the Protestant ethic). In the south, the enjoyment of life is more important; you work to live. The Mediterranean attitude is: well, maybe we have spent too much but we can repent and start again (the Catholic view).

Another factor in the decline of Europe is the lack of population growth and hence relatively shrinking markets, but this will be partly offset by an influx of displaced people from North Africa and the Middle East. He says a city like Birmingham will have a majority Muslim population by 2020. Dealing with Russia, he says it is a mess, with half the defence budget disappearing because of corruption and such a high turnover of skilled manpower that they can hardly keep their weapons systems going. It is an interesting talk but rather US-centric. Later, at dinner, Roger and Carol say it is as if the talk was prepared for an American audience.

The lecture ends at 11am and I decide it is not yet warm enough for shorts. It is a strange day for these latitudes, but I suppose we are still in the northern hemisphere winter, and we have only just entered the tropics by crossing the Tropic of Cancer. I visit the shops in the Grand Lobby area: you can get what you want but the prices are high. I go back to the Illuminations lobby for the 1pm movie and see the director Hugh Hudson sitting outside talking to a guest.

I move in when he is free and tell him my story about the brain haemorrhage suffered by my wife, and he says eagerly: "Is she here?" I explain why not and he looks disappointed but advises me to speak to his wife Maryam about it. She is going to introduce the movie *Rupture* when it is screened. I go on to tell him how much I enjoyed *Chariots of Fire*, setting the stage for a tradition of British period features. I mention *Downton Abbey* and he expresses disdain.

In the auditorium he introduces his movie *My Life So Far* (1999). It was shot entirely in Scotland on the shores of Loch Fyne near Glasgow and features amateur child actors plucked out of the local population. "They are delightful and fresh and come with no pretensions, so there is a wonderful air of innocence that comes through in their acting," he says. It is a thoroughly charming movie about a young boy of about 11 who is part of a large family with a lovely child-centred Dad played by Colin Firth.

The boy is at that stage of development where he is exploring what sex is about, and whether there is another sort of music besides his father's beloved Beethoven that gets drilled into him. A young relative gives him a Louis Armstrong record which he plays in secret. He wants to learn more about the world because his father does not give satisfactory answers. He reads Uncle Macintosh's books which no one else has opened and finds saucy prints of unclothed women hidden between the pages. At the end when he is late coming to church his father goes back to check and finds his young son with feet up, listening to Louis Armstrong, looking at saucy pictures and smoking a cigar. Wisely, his father closes the door and leaves him to it.

In the Q&A afterwards, Hugh says it was distributed by Miramax who were promoting *Cider House Rules* with Michael Caine at the same time. They consequently neglected to push his movie and it did not do well at the box office. He thinks it a great pity, but philosophically puts it down to the politics of the movie industry.

I have lunch on Deck 7, this time a sort of healthy one – lettuce and tuna salad. I see a pile of peaches on the buffet and have one for dessert. It is ripe and juicy and after that I am always looking out for a peach in the fruit bowls. I go back to Illuminations to the lecture about the sinking of the Russian submarine *Kursk* in August 2000. The talk is given by a Master Mariner called Captain John Nixon who is a marine insurance and salvage expert. He is a big, bluff, no nonsense fellow. He describes what happened with slides and then turns to speculating why it happened.

The submarine was on manoeuvres in the Barents Sea. It successfully fired a missile and was then to fire a torpedo when things went wrong. There was a small explosion in the bow followed by a very large one which catastrophically ruptured the hull and sank the ship. There were 23 survivors trapped in the rear compartment but they died before they could be rescued. A device called a rescue pod could have saved them but it too was damaged. Nixon says back in 1939 submariners were rescued from a disaster with a type of pod that was then in use, so there was no excuse for one not working 60 years later.

He has three theories of what caused the explosions. Either the torpedo blew up in the torpedo tube when the launch button was pressed, or after launch the torpedo boomeranged back and hit the submarine – there was a hole the size of a torpedo in the skin of the hull. The third theory he considers most unlikely – but which the Russians promoted – that a US submarine in the area fired a torpedo which sank the *Kursk*. Somebody knows what happened but the Russians aren't talking. Numerous conspiracy theory books, mostly fanciful, have been published to cash in on the mystery.

The lecture finishes at 4.15pm so I have time to relax. I decide to send a joint text message to my sons from their sailor Dad. "Off bulge of Africa, great food drink entertainment and no supervision!" Earlier Lucy sent me a message "Good morning Grandpa! Amelie wanted to confirm you've reached warm waters now? Did you eat a banana in Tenerife? Hope you are having fun." I reply to tell Amelie, my granddaughter, I'm hoping to see flying fish. The boys respond to my message with words like awesome and tremendous. Guy says it sounds like "Man Heaven" which is a good way of describing my situation. I feel happily connected with the world to be able to exchange short messages.

I shower and dress for dinner. It is the first semi-formal night so I get to wear familiar jacket and tie. I go to the Chartroom bar on Deck 3 outside the Britannia restaurant for a pre-dinner drink. A string quartet made up of four attractive young women is playing soothing classical music to an appreciative audience at the tables and sofas round the room. The large picture windows show the sea streaming past. I take a stool at the bar so that I can see the room, the sea and the quartet.

I order a Bombay Sapphire gin Martini straight up with an olive. This delicious concoction gives you a full strength feeling of elation. The bar person enquires how my day was and sets down a plate of canapes for me, four tasty morsels each skewered with a toothpick. Whenever I have a Martini I am reminded of my youngest son Roger's shrewd advice from Hendrik, his administrator at work in Vancouver, who tells the young bucks gathered at the bar: "You shouldn't start the evening with a Martini, boys; you'll take off like a helicopter. Better to drink something that puts you into a gentle glide." At my age I prefer the helicopter.

The quartet is very good, the guests are all smartly turned out and the scene is just perfect. I think there are a lot of well heeled, successful and well educated people on board spending their money. Some of the questions and comments at the Q&As after the talks I've been to are obviously from people who are at home in the wide world. I feel like another Martini because it was so good, but it is time to go to dinner.

I am first at the table as this time I have brought my appetite. I can choose where to sit. Roger and Carol and Margaret join me but the Canadians give the restaurant a miss tonight. We talk about what we did all day; Roger and Carol have been to the talks I went to and the Hugh Hudson movie. Now we have been dining together for a while we have shifted to the easy familiarity of small talk. Margaret tells a story of how she had her handbag stolen when she arrived jet lagged at a New York hotel.

Still dressed up, I go to the Illuminations theatre for the fourth time in one day for my second movie, *Super 8*. This refers to the inexpensive Kodak camera that made home movies easy in the 1970s. It is a Steven Spielberg confection made in 1979 about a group of teens making movies as a hobby for summer holidays and they accidently film a train crash that is inexplicable. Until halfway through, the show is credible and entertaining and I enjoy the American teen dialogue which reminds me of the quips and exchanges between the boys in my son Roger's Little League baseball team. But the movie turns into a ridiculous science fiction story that gets more and more improbable until it is so bad I feel ashamed to be watching such trash.

After that I am off to bed, feeling pleasantly tired. I read the news digest delivered when Dong turns down the bed. Shadow chancellor Ed Balls is in trouble with the unions for saying Labour won't rescind the government pay cuts in the public service. Rio Tinto stock is back at £35 which is encouraging. The Greek bailout agreement is heading for the rocks as a two speed Euro economy looms. So all is normal then.

I go to sleep with only a slight sensation of the movement of the ship ploughing its way southward on a calm sea.

Monday 16 January

At Sea. Noon position 13N 17W

I wake up at 6am without the alarm clock and shave and get dressed. I decide I will have breakfast in the Britannia restaurant so I put on smart trousers. I go downstairs for a cup of tea on Deck 7. Dennis is in his usual place eating a cooked breakfast on cue and reading the *Daily Programme*. He says he had a cold when he left England and it went away but now it is back. I shift my chair backwards a bit. We talk about the lectures and movies from yesterday.

He saw *Super 8* but came in half way so only saw the rubbish bit. I tell him about the Russian submarine story. I don't think he will be interested in the evolution of international relations in the 21st century so I tell him about Hugh Hudson and his movies and how I had a chat with him about *Rupture*. I explain why I am interested as my wife had a brain haemorrhage. He is surprised and affected by it. I have finished my tea and he his breakfast so we move on. Apparently he is reluctant to use the Britannia restaurant because he is alone, but I encourage him, saying solo people aren't treated any differently. Ironically, when I go to breakfast, for the first and only time I am seated alone at a table for two. No matter, I am content in my own company and don't have to make conversation.

At 10am I go to the Illuminations theatre again to hear the second lecture on the Russian nuclear submarine *Kursk*, about the salvage operation. Captain Nixon tells us that because the disaster caused such a public outcry, with allegations of incompetence by the military, President Vladimir Putin rather rashly promised to salvage the submarine and bring the bodies home to their families for burial.

This was a very difficult salvage operation, with all the technology and equipment having to be purpose designed, built and deployed from scratch in a matter of months for the salvage to take place in the late summer of 2001 (the disaster had occurred in August 2000). Two Dutch firms were employed, with Nixon acting as consultant to one of them. The shattered bow had to be cut off because it posed a danger to the raising of the hull from 100m below the surface, and anyway the Russians didn't want anyone to see it in case it revealed military secrets.

So a way had to be devised to cut off the shattered bow. This was done with a specially invented system of saws operated by cables moving to and fro from structures fastened to the seabed on either side. It took a week to saw off the bow. They then drilled holes along the top of the hull and inserted vertical cables fastened on the same principle as those fastener screws that open like wings behind wallboard. The cables from the top of the submarine went vertically through the bottom of the specially made salvage barge so that the submarine remained upright to keep its nuclear reactor stable.

The lifting operation was successful, with the submarine nestling under the hull of the barge while it was towed to dry dock. Because with the sub underneath the draught of the barge was too deep to enter dry dock, special pontoons were built to raise the barge and the submarine high enough out of the water to get into the dock. The bodies were recovered and the hull was investigated. The conning tower was saved as a memorial and the rest of the submarine went to a secret scrapyard in Siberia.

An insight into the Russian mind was given by the fact that the deputy head of the navy signed a letter ensuring, for the purpose of the salvage companies' insurance, that there were no nuclear weapons on board the submarine. Of course no nuclear submarine would leave port without nuclear weapons and indeed they were found to be on board once the ship was in dry dock.

There is a short break and soon I am back for the second lecture by Ambassador Howard Walker on the 21st century international order. This time he talks exclusively about the US and its continuing role as the greatest country on Earth. As he said before, the US will continue to be a superpower but with the rise of China, not *the* superpower. He says the US defence budget is equal to the combined value of the rest of the world's defence budgets put together.

The US leads in ideas, concepts and innovation which are more value adding than manufacturing and assembly, which have gone offshore. For example, Apple gets a 36 per cent profit on an iPad and the company in China that assembles them makes a profit of only two per cent. Nevertheless, US manufacturing is not to be sneezed at and is growing with the repatriation of offshore jobs. BMW has opened a plant in North

Virginia which pays wages below those paid to BMW workers in Germany. The US accepts this in the interests of gaining jobs for its citizens. The downsides to the US are common to other countries, mainly unsustainable debt which will have to be funded, and "pockets of low educational achievement coupled to the growth of a permanent underclass".

My brain having been exercised for the day, I start on recreation by going outside for the first time. The sea is deep blue, fairly calm and there is a great deal of white water roiling along the port side. I missed most of the Commodore's noon talk but see the details on the bulletin board by the pool on Deck 12. We are off The Gambia, towards the bottom of the bulge of Africa. We are nearing the equator and have sailed 933 miles from Tenerife with 2,889 miles to go to Walvis Bay. The speed is 21 knots (24 mph), the water is 10,000ft deep and the air temperature 25C.

I go to my cabin. Dong is changing the sheets. He tells me he changes the sheets every three days which I tell him is very generous. When he is gone I change into my swim shorts and go to the pool. I settle down on a lounger out of direct sunlight and relax before having a swim when the pool is clear. Once out and dried, I signal a steward and he brings me a Bass. Later I go out of the glass doors on to the deck for a walk. From the Deck 12 level there are steps up to the Deck 13 sundeck area, the size of the Prairies,where you really feel you're in the great outdoors.

At lunch in the Britannia restaurant I am seated beside a man and his wife who I have seen at the lectures.

They are from Sudbury, Ontario and he says he retired recently from the position of chief executive of the Sudbury Science Centre. I tell him about my background in mining and a visit I once made to his town. We find we have quite a lot in common as the nickel mining centre of Sudbury is all Falconbridge and Inco, now Xstrata and Vale following mergers and acquisitions. The Science Centre got its start from a generous donation from Inco.

The couple took the *QM2* from New York two weeks ago and are going to Cape Town for a holiday before visiting the Kruger Park on the way home. They are pleased to be escaping the Northern Ontario winter. He tells me he has just downsized his house and they now have one of 1,500sq ft which sounds like the size of the house we had in North Vancouver. They also have a "cottage" in the wilds north east of Sudbury in a place that is not on the electrical grid.

After lunch I am on the Observation deck with my camera and binoculars hoping to see something interesting in the sea. With my binoculars pointed skywards I spot two flapping birds. We are out of sight of land, or maybe at their height they can see land, though I doubt it. They are large, brown coloured birds with a massive wingspan. They look like giant cranes or pelicans.

They are flying on the same course as the ship and seem to be gaining on us, then they start to turn and swoop back in the opposite direction, turning and resuming their flight in the same direction the ship is going.

They do this a couple of times as if they are tired of flying against the wind and turn for relief. Finally they do their backwards swoop and disappear round the back of the ship away from the direction of land and I do not see them again. This rather boring encounter is my only wildlife sighting of the whole trip: no dolphins, no flying fish.

I go down and shower and change into my dinner jacket. I have trouble with fastening the bow tie again. Because the mirror shows the opposite of what you have to do I just can't make my fingers do it. Eventually I am all dickied up. I rig up a way of balancing my camera on a towel rail in the bathroom, where the light is brightest and I don't need the flash, setting the timer and taking a picture of myself reflected in the mirror. Considering the rubbish that passes for art these days this picture may earn me a quirky award.

I repeat my pre-dinner drink routine in the Chartroom, sitting in the same place and ordering the same Martini from the same bar person. Her name is Lena and she is from Belarus. It is hard to follow what she is saying. I tell her about the *Kursk* submarine lecture but this is a mistake. She misunderstands my drift and goes on crossly and defensively about how important it is for a country to defend itself, even with submarines. The music is provided by a harpist who is not as uplifting as the string quartet and she stops early. I finish my drink at 6pm and go through to the restaurant.

The Canadians are no-shows again so it is Roger, Carol and Margaret. I discover that Roger and Carol live in

Woking, only a few miles from Farnham. I had asked them where home is, by way of making conversation, and Roger replied: "I'm sure you've never heard of it but it is a place called Woking which is somewhere near London." They are equally surprised when I tell them I live in Farnham, which they say they sometimes visit to shop.

We swop stories about how we ended up where we did. They had moved from Aberdeen where Roger was in the offshore oil industry. He considers his move to be of the same scale as a foreign move like mine from Canada. Margaret tells an amusing story about how she committed to buy their house without first telling her husband. From the menu, the others choose surf and turf – lobster and steak, and I have pork loin which is tender. I skip the wine because I plan to watch football and that involves beer.

The others have been invited to a Commodore's cocktail party so I go to the Golden Lion pub for the football. The screen has the coloured stripes waiting for the satellite transmission. Everyone keeps asking, where is the game? The barman explains that the channel is just kept open and picks up the football when the feed starts so they have no control over it. It comes on okay. Here we are far away on the ocean waves in the tropic zone, watching 22 men playing a ball game in the freezing fog of Wigan, Lancashire. It is Manchester City, who are top of the league, against Wigan Athletic, who are bottom. Manchester City have a bad night and win by only one goal, fluffing several chances.

Back in my cabin after 10pm, I undress, dealing with more obstruction from the bow tie, and lie in bed reading the *Daily Programme* for tomorrow. There is a classical piano recital that I would like to go to and a presentation by Maryam d'Abo introducing a short film she made on the "Bond girls", the women who have played opposite James Bond.

The schedule has an amazing variety of activities and is typical of what is on offer every day of the cruise. One can have a holiday of a lifetime with opportunities like these; not to mention the food, drink and the beautiful sea stretching in all directions, plus visiting different places on ports of call. But I must concede that an uninterrupted three months of this, 108 nights from 10 January to 27 April, the full Monty world voyage, could turn these positives upside down. Once you've done everything several times or more, it may start seeming like prison.

Tuesday 17 January

At Sea. Noon position 6N 13W

I put on shorts and go on Deck 13. Opening the door to the weather I feel the warm humid wind of the tropics. I can feel the ship interior is much cooler due to the air conditioning. It is still dark at 6.40am, the sun is due to come up at 7am. In the tropics the light comes suddenly. I take a walk round the deck and then go down to have tea on Deck 7. Dennis approaches at the tea and coffee dispenser. He is looking sunburned and says his cold is worse and full blown so I should keep away.

I have Shredded Wheat with my tea and a banana, although I am tempted by the smoked fish and scrambled eggs at the buffet. Dennis does not seem to go to many events so I tell him about the salvage of the Russian submarine. His news is that he enquired at the booking desk for future cruises about going to Singapore on the QM2 via Suez when she embarks on another world voyage the other way round in 2013. They quoted $7,000 so he is thinking about it. This is a solo fare on Deck 6 which has balconies. I tell him about my upgrade for this cruise which was offered voluntarily by Cunard and he is quite surprised. He says it is all luck of the draw as to when you book that results in the deal you get. He knows someone who booked a month or so before departure and received a good deal.

I go to Deck 13 and walk round the perimeter a couple of times. It is better than doing the Deck 7 circuit because there are fewer people, and there are a number of stairways to make it slightly more energetic. The only drawback is that the railings are double height so you don't get a good view of the sea. There are smoked-glass panels at head height on top of the regular railing and you have to stop and peek through a gap to see the sea properly.

In my cabin I check my phone which I keep in the safe with my passport, wallet and computer, and see S has just sent a text noting I've been gone a week and she is well but the weather is very cold. I send her a text saying we are off the coast of Sierra Leone and cross the equator tomorrow. I describe conditions as warm and humid, flat sea, hazy visibility. I also send my sister Val a text of our progress and tell her I plan to disembark a day early, the 24th, rather than the 25th. That is next Tuesday – only a week left. Val acknowledges, saying she is glad I will be a day early; I must just phone and they will pick me up.

I spend the morning walking and relaxing on deck. I do more circuits of the perimeter of Deck 13, then find some shade to lie on a lounger. It is hot and humid and most people lie out in the direct sun with no protection. It is hard to understand what pleasure they feel under the burning sun and later they will surely have serious sunburns. I find reflected light is quite strong enough for me. Feeling hot, I go and change into my swim shorts and go to the pool. There are surprisingly few people. The roof is closed, probably to keep in the air conditioned cool. I read my Churchill book for a while then go for a swim. The water is lovely and cool. The pool is quite small so when there are four others I get out.

The noon report says we have travelled 516 miles in the last 24 hours, 1,449 miles from Tenerife. It is 2,378 miles to Walvis Bay. The speed is 22 knots and there is 13,700 ft of water under the keel. The air and water temperature are almost the same at 28C and 27C respectively. Sunrise and sunset have also become almost equal; sunrise was 6.56am this morning and sunset will be 6.44pm this evening. We are in the equilibrium of the equator and even the winds cancel each other out. This is the doldrums, where sailing ships became becalmed and just drifted aimlessly. The *QM2* ploughs on, churning the blue ocean into a white maelstrom along its sides.

I get back into my shorts and go to lunch at the King's Court buffet. I have cottage pie and broccoli followed by an orange and a peach. I have to wander about looking for a place to sit, but I am quite comfortable being alone. There are dozens of people on their own, either solo travellers or more likely couples doing their thing separately. So there is no shame in sitting alone, a factor that worried me a bit before the cruise. I revel in my independence but wish S was here to enjoy it as much as I do.

I go to the Royal Court theatre for a piano recital by Allan Schiller, who is a leading British pianist. He comes from Leeds in Yorkshire and was trained in Moscow. He riffles along with an expert rendition of Beethoven's *Moonlight Sonata* as his main feature. It is very relaxing. There is a couple of my generation sitting below me in the stalls (I am in the front row of the balcony) who are nestled up against each other like teenagers at a music festival. His arm is around her and she has her hand on his bare forearm. Most couples on the ship appear to continue the routine domestic habits of home, a rather stiff and undemonstrative companionship. These two show the affection of a couple who value every day. She even gives him a quick kiss after he speaks to her. That's the way to go, before time takes it all away.

Love is in the air because the next piece of entertainment is the short film made for TV by Maryam d'Abo on the many women who have played in the James Bond films, of whom she is one. Her documentary *Bond Girls are Forever* involved interviewing the women about their roles, and tracing the changes in social attitudes they embody from the 1960s to the present. In the first Bond films women were ornamental sex objects: now they fight, kick and gun down the bad guys alongside James Bond. Maryam interviews 15 leading ladies from the 20 Bond films so far, including the first, Ursula Andress in *Dr No*, and Honor Blackman who was Pussy Galore in *Goldfinger*.

It is the sort of "people behind the movie" interviews that S would have enjoyed. Maryam was herself a Bond girl playing in *The Living Daylights* which is not a movie I have heard of. She is British in origin but lived internationally with her parents. She could not get anyone in the UK interested in financing her idea for the Bond girls documentary so she went to America and raised the money right away. She stayed in the US for ten years so is little known in the UK as an actress or film maker. She says only in America could she have switched from actor to director; it doesn't happen in Britain – it's a closed shop dominated by males.

At the end of the Q&A she refers to the film *Rupture* which will be screened later this week, about her emotional journey set off by a brain injury. She calls it a movie with a positive message about the strength of the life force. She adds that it is to be shown on BBC4 in England later in the year.

I go back to my cabin and get ready for dinner. This is a semi-formal night so it is easy enough to put on a clean shirt and tie. I go to the Chartroom for a drink and have a caipirinha cocktail from Brazil – rum, lemon and sugar in crushed ice. The crushed ice lowers the octane level but it's still a good choice and I enjoy it with the music from the string quartet. The sun is sinking towards the sea in the west, blazing dazzling reflections from the water into the cocktail lounge.

All six are present at dinner; Joe and Leo get there first. They say they went to Todd English last night as guests: that's the fine dining restaurant for which you have to pay extra. We talk about the capsizing of the Italian ship *Costa Concordia* on the coast of Italy. It has all been on the TV news broadcast in our cabins, which I haven't been watching. The ship belongs to Carnival Lines company Costa Crociere and Carnival's stock has plummeted in the US. Several people have been killed, others are missing and more injured. It seems the captain may have been making an unauthorised visit to an island when the ship hit the rocks and keeled over on its side. He left the ship while there were still passengers on board and there is a recording of the Coastguard angrily telling him to get back aboard his ship. Now he is under house arrest.

Carol tells me she went to line dancing and met a lady who comes from Alton, near Farnham, so with Margaret from Fareham, the Surrey/Hampshire area is well represented. The conversation turns to who has visited the war graves in Normandy and northern France. Leo seems to be quite an authority as he has done it all, including of course Vimy Ridge, the Canadian memorial. Roger is writing a book about the Commonwealth War Graves Commission's work and tracing the lives of servicemen from the First World War whose names are inscribed on the war memorial in their home village. Joe leaves the table early: he has been quiet and seems to be in work mode. Leo tells me he has just conducted a memorial service on board attended by the Filipino crew for the loss of one of their own in an off-ship accident in the Philippines over Christmas.

Before I go to bed I put my watch and bedside clock forward one hour. South Africa is two hours ahead of England at this time of year so we will have to do it once more before Walvis Bay. Dong had reminded me of the change by leaving the television on with instructions on the screen. Dong leaves two bedtime chocolates on my bed each night. I started saving one for S and eating the other; now I save both so I have quite a stash of goodnight treats. They come in dark, milk, mint and orange in a Cunard wrapper.

Chapter 3

Equator

Wednesday 18 January

At Sea. Noon position 00 19S 7W

I get up, shave and dress at 6.30am and go to the Observation deck. It is still dark with black storm clouds and a strong but warm breeze peppered with raindrops. There is a robust sea coursing from the west on the open ocean side. We are now running south east having passed the bulge and heading across the "armpit" of Africa to Walvis Bay on the south west coast.

The Deck 13 planking is coloured dark from the rain and is being soaked again with hoses as the deck crews do a dawn wash down with rubber sweepers. Every late afternoon the deck crews, who wear neat khaki long trousers and white T-shirts with baseball caps, clear the decks by collecting all the loungers, stacking and lashing them up attached to a railing so they are secure for the night and won't slide about. Each morning they laboriously unstack them, and lay them out in neat rows for the sun worshippers, only to have to put them away again in the evening. It's a wearisome job but to me an indication of good seamanship and safety awareness – all "shipshape and Bristol fashion".

Below on Deck 7 the wooden deck chairs (same design as on the *Titanic*) are left where they are for the night facing the sea but the footrests are all turned up. The cushions are kept in big wooden trunks against the bulkheads and are brought out for the day. The crews laboriously tie the tapes of each back and bottom cushion to the chair so the cushions do not blow away. The storage boxes themselves are kept beautifully varnished and you can sit on them, look at the sea and have a beverage you have brought out from the adjacent buffet.

I go below to have coffee and breakfast on Deck 7. I join Dennis who says he is sure the air conditioning is the cause of his cold. He stayed out of his cabin all yesterday and felt better but after a night of being in the air conditioning again he is stuffed up. We talk about a 3D movie that was shown last night which he says was packed out even though it was a kids' movie. Second childhood? This leads to talk about 3D television. He says his area of Britain doesn't even have HD television yet.

I ask him where he lives and it turns out to be Hove in Sussex – so another near neighbour. He lives alone and seems to travel a lot to get away from the English winter. He likes his drinks and is surprised when I tell him I am the only one at our dinner table who ever has wine. He says he might have five or six drinks a day. I tell him I set myself a budget of £50 a day but am not coming close to that. He laughs and says that is the exactly the amount he set himself. He says he went to the disco last night to have a look. He was surprised to see that there were very few people, about six couples, and, even more improbably, they were elderly and not exactly dancing up a storm. Anyway, credit to them for showing up. I had gone to bed.

After I've had coffee and Dennis has left I serve myself smoked fish and an omelette with a slice of buttered bread. I finish with a pink grapefruit half. It is segmented so you can scoop it out of the skin. On the way out on deck I stop at the television monitors – one is from Cunard and shows rolling screens of our position in latitude and longitude, miles travelled, sea and air temperatures and a map of our course with the ship's position.

There are screens for Sky News and BBC World and an American channel which is showing a political discussion on Newt Gingrich. Sky and BBC are going big on the Italian ship disaster with reporters on the spot. There are 11 dead and 20 unaccounted for. The captain is in big trouble. The story will raise awareness of the theoretical dangers of cruising just when I am on a cruise, but I feel quite safe.

I go out on deck, it is grey and windy and a storm is coming towards us from the open sea side – which stretches all the way to Brazil. Waves break with a roar against the starboard side as the ship muscles its way through the water with no concessions to the pressures of the currents; there's no up or down motion. A dark cloud is discharging a curtain of grey rain and the wind disturbs the surface of the sea. I wait and watch it approaching from the shelter of a steel overhang among the lifeboats.

When the rain hits us it patters on the deck but seems to make no impression on the surface of the ocean. You can't see it spotting the surface like you do with a lake or a puddle. For the sea a rainstorm must be a piddling addition of water, literally a drop in the ocean. The walkers round Deck 7 continue to stride along in the brief downpour, allowing themselves to get soaked. I am getting damp from the fine mist of droplets blowing on to me so I go inside and hang out my shirt to dry. It is noticeably cold when you come inside to the air conditioning.

I go on a mission to find out how far we are from the equator by looking at the information screen of the televisions on Deck 7. It says we are 00deg 30mins N, so not far to the line. I also look for the cabin S and I occupied on our trip to New York in 2006, No. 6187 on Deck 6. The door is closed and of course looks like all the others except that it has a hanger saying "Make up Room". It is close to a bank of elevators so it must have been convenient for us to get around.

When the weather is clear I go on deck. I am doing a circuit to see where the Crossing the Line ceremony will be when I come across Dennis. I tap my watch and say "equator time". He has a backpack with his camera and says the ceremony is at 12.30pm. It is funny that we are comfortable with each other's company each morning, but meeting on the deck we become awkward and want to get away. Must be a "Man Thing"; women would not be like that.

The Commodore gives us a five minute warning and we cross into the southern hemisphere at 10.45am (9.45am GMT). The equator is an imaginary line equidistant from the North Pole and the South Pole and divides the northern and southern hemispheres. It is 0 degrees and the only line of latitude that is also a "great circle", i.e. spanning the whole circumference of the earth. It is the only place on earth where night and day are always the same length.

In *Journey to Java* Nicolson's wife Vita sweetly asked the captain of the MV *Willem Ruys* why there was not a string of coloured buoys to mark the location of the equator. She needed to see it, to actualise the crossing from one half of the globe to the other. The pragmatic sea captain said it would be rather difficult to set up and maintain a line of buoys round the circumference of the Earth. Yet it is a concept we can all relate to. You look out to sea and say: now I wonder where exactly is the equator? I decide since what you see from a ship is an infinitesimal patch compared to the scale of a map, I can safely assume that within my range of sight I can see the equator.

The Crossing the Line ceremony is to take place beside the pool on the aft deck at 12.30pm, as Dennis said. For some reason connected with my innumeracy I misread my watch and go to reserve a viewing spot at the rail at 11am, thinking it is 12 noon and a short while to go. So I am *really* early as I wait one and a half hours for the thing to start. It isn't all that bad. The tropical rainshowers have spiralled away, the sun is out, and the sea under a clear sky turns a glorious deep blue with gentle swells. Looking aft you can see the broad wake left by the ship churning the surface into a flat, mangled mixture of aquamarine and white.

The deck where the ceremony is to take place is part of the premium Princess Grill section which is off limits to us Britannia Grill passengers. The stewards set out chairs and a stand bearing the Cunard logo to sell champagne from huge silver punchbowls filled with ice cubes to accommodate a dozen bottles each. We can only watch, though of course if you could find one of the roaming stewards they would bring you champagne. I notice few people actually have straight champagne; they order mixtures – champagne with a dash of kir or a shot of Drambuie and orange juice topped with champagne. Rather a waste of the lovely bubbly, I think to myself. With the sun hot, the sea blue, the people happy, and the ship on the equator, what is there not to like?

The *Daily Programme* says of the day's events: "The Crossing the Line ceremony owes its origin to ancient pagan rites connected with the propitiation of the Greek sea god Poseidon, known to the Romans as Neptune. In classical times it was the custom to mark the rounding of a significant headland by making a sacrificial offering to the appropriate deity. In more recent times, the ceremony as we see it today was originally regarded as a test for seasoned sailors to ensure that their new shipmates were capable of handling long, rough trips to sea. In modern times sailors who have already 'crossed the line' are nicknamed Shellbacks, and those who haven't are known as Pollywogs."

Harold Nicolson, the learned classicist, had difficulty with the Crossing the Line ceremony. He wrote in *Journey to Java*: "*In the* Willem Ruys *the ceremony of crossing the line is celebrated with customary cordiality . . . I was displeased by this partly because I have a profound reverence for the more elderly Olympians and shall not enjoy seeing Poseidon (who after all was the son of Saturn and own brother to Zeus himself) being treated as a comic character. When at breakfast I explained to V. my apprehensions regarding the impending ceremony she reproved me for being snooty and for having no sense of fun.*"

At 12 noon the Commodore makes his eight bells announcement on progress. We are now off the coast of Liberia, our position is just south of the equator at 00deg 19mins S. Our speed is 21 knots; we have travelled 503 miles in the last 24 hours and are 1,956 miles from Tenerife and have 1,870 miles to go to Walvis Bay, where we will arrive on Sunday, 22 January at 7.30am. There is 16,500ft of water (three miles) under the ship and the air and sea temperature are the same at 26C.

The railings are filled with people and my view of the pool area has become obscured by people gathering at the rail on the next level down. Latecomers look mystified that there is a press of people three deep along the railings. I feel sorry for an elderly couple who must be in their mid-eighties, who, moving rather unsteadily, emerge on deck and looking around, find there is no place to gain a vantage point. Standing on a lounger is not an option for them.

A few days ago they called for volunteers to be Pollywogs. They easily get the 25 people needed. Why anyone would put their hand up is beyond me. Maybe they have a sense of self loathing, or it means a lot to be featured on the cruise video that comes on sale. It involves being humiliated by having slops from the kitchen smeared over the body then jumping in the pool to wash it off. In times gone by, sailors were smeared with the filth and waste from the bilges of the ship.

The ceremony starts with the entrance of Neptune and his "court" – a queen and attendants, with Neptune holding a trident and wearing robes and long grey beard. Amusing declarations are read in rhyming couplets alluding to the prosecution of the Pollywogs who have failed to do this or that, or, to make it contemporary, have questioned their drinks bill. The Commodore reads out a rhyming welcome to Neptune requesting that permission be granted to cross the line. The Engineering Officer expresses sorrow that all the slops are going to end up in the pool which he is responsible for cleaning, and the officer who is Hotel Manager bewails the fact that everyone will be late for lunch today.

After further pronouncements, the spectators are asked if they agree the Pollywogs are guilty and should be punished. A shout of yes goes up. The 25 volunteers lie down in turn on a table and are smeared with liquidised matter in green, yellow and brown. There is a faint garbage truck smell of food waste. They then shower or get in the pool to general cheers and merriment.

Feeling hot after standing so long in the sun I head for my cabin and change into my swim shorts for an equatorial dip in the pool. I order a Bass from Edgardo, settle down out of the direct sun and relax before taking a swim. The entertainment staff have organised a table tennis tournament. It is a knockout round robin with the first games being played the best of 21 points so that if you are knocked out in the first round you still get a fair game. The players await their turn. One very intense bald-headed fellow is losing and you can see he so badly wants to win. He constantly verbalises his feelings. The other chap is a cool customer and doesn't show any emotion or say anything, he just steadily wins. I reflect on this as a lesson for getting ahead in life; keep your cool.

On a trip to the library I borrow a book *The Smell of the Continent* by two Oxford historians, James Munson and Richard Mullen. It is about the heyday of British travel to Europe between 1814, the end of the Napoleonic wars, and 1914, just before the First World War. I take it to my cabin to read. The book shows that the British have always been inveterate travellers, escaping with curiosity from the confines of their island to see what other countries are like. In Victorian times, unique among the nations of Europe, they had the wealth to do so. The British invented tourism; what began as a luxury for the rich, became in time the fashion for the middle class.

The rising prosperity of Victorian England meant that middle class tourists travelling on the newly built railways could visit the Rhine for £3. Mass tourism was under way by 1850, partly driven by a fact that we are familiar with today – holidays in England cost nearly twice as much as those on the Continent. A whole culture grew up around travel guidebooks, maintaining households in Italy and visits to the Alps and the Rhine. Wherever they went the visitors demanded improvements in the standards of accommodation, meals and sanitation, to match amenities they were used to at home. If they had negative experiences they would write indignant letters to *The Times*. The Continentals who made improvements to satisfy the British tourists met with the greatest commercial success. The British kept journals of their travels and made fun of one another.

He next proceeds to Chamouni [sic] *and up Mont Blanc*
    he climbs,
And coming back, of course, he writes a letter to The Times.
In fact, he climbs up anything, without an aim or view
Because he has a notion it's the sort of thing to do.

Writers noted that tourists on the Rhine looked down at their guidebooks lying open on their laps and read the descriptions of the very towns and castles that were passing by, scarcely lifting their eyes to the real scenes, except now and then to observe that it is "very nice". The British had to have passports to enter Europe because Europeans had to have "passes" to move about within their own countries (like black people under apartheid). Police stopped everyone for their papers and to examine their luggage for contraband. They often gave the British a hard time, locking them up if something was amiss. Of course the freedom loving British hated this as there had never been any hindrance to them moving about their own country and this applied to visitors to Britain as well.

In the present age, tourism is clearly still in the English blood; this voyage is further proof of it, except of course conditions and places to go have improved and grown exponentially. The 1,650 British on board the *QM2* outnumber all the other 27 nationalities combined. But this is only the first leg to Cape Town. The position may be reversed to an antipodean majority when the ship is making a circumnavigation of Australia in February.

I get ready for dinner. It is a formal night with Neptune's Ball the main feature. I manage the bow tie okay and go to the Chartroom for a pre-dinner drink. The formidable Lena of Belarus is behind the bar, trying to explain to an earnest British couple where her country is located. She is careful to emphasise it is not part of Russia. I order a Bombay Sapphire Martini and she mixes it very well. I am a bit late so my intake is rather more rapid than I would have liked.

At table Joe and Leo ask the wine waiter to retrieve a bottle of sparkling wine that was given to them during the trip from New York to Southampton and which was deposited with a steward serving at another table. (You can buy wine by the bottle and it can be kept for you and brought out each evening.) The steward comes back to say both the bottle and the steward are not there. The steward left the ship at Southampton and no one knows what happened to the bottle.

I have turkey. There is too much meat and not enough to go with it. I suspect the potato was left off in error. I mention it to Alex and he/she promises to investigate but I hear no more. The wine steward comes back towards the end of our main course and says the chief wine steward has provided a bottle of sparkling wine free of charge. It is the same Pol Aker complimentary wine provided in my cabin when I boarded. We each have a glass and it gives a friendly buzz, though coming at the wrong time in the sequence of food and drink.

I take the opportunity to talk to Joe who is seated beside me about the Ambassador's remarks on Protestant Germans versus Catholic Mediterraneans with their belief in repentance. I want an explanation of the theological basis of repentance. To me it seems as if it makes it okay to be bad. Joe is probably no theologian as he just laughs and blusters, talking about the time he met the Ambassador and what an interesting guy he is.

I still wonder whether, theologically speaking, the concept of being able to repent and start over (and therefore in theory resume bad ways) lies at the heart of the difference between Protestantism and Catholicism. In the Middle Ages it was the scandal of priests and others (Pardoners) selling "indulgences" (which supposedly forgave sins) that led to the German Martin Luther's break from the Catholic Church and the start of Protestantism.

After the meal I go to the Photo Gallery to see if I can get a digital file of the picture of me with the Commodore, taken the first formal night out of Southampton. The South African-accented girl can't help: she wants only to sell me the print for $25 which sounds expensive or a "package" I don't want. The pettiness annoys me. I try the movie in Illuminations: *Dead Again*, another Kenneth Branagh film. I settle down and watch the first ten minutes and decide it is not for me, with too much swearing and swanking about; Branagh playing an American is embarrassing.

I leave and walk up the staircases in the front of the ship from Deck 3 to Deck 8 to the Commodore Club, a very smart cocktail bar looking out over the bows of the ship. It is packed with cool glitterati couples all dressed up for the ball. There is no place to park myself, not even standing at the bar. Feeling stared at, my confidence ebbs and I head on out. As I do so I pass and greet the man and his wife from Sudbury, Ontario. I think to myself later I should have paused, relaxed and sat down with them for a while and had a glass and conversation. Like many married couples they were just sitting in companionable silence, having a cocktail before probably going to the Neptune Ball.

So with three strike-outs on a dress-up night it is not a stellar evening. Back in my cabin, on my mobile there is a message from S that has just come in saying she had a busy day in Dorking and is off to bed early. I am glad I am there to reply before she turns in. I say I am doing the same. Then she sends another text saying she has completed the rigmarole of booking our accommodation in Vancouver for our youngest son Roger's wedding in August.

On the bed with the daily news digest and schedule of activities for tomorrow, there is an ornate certificate from Cunard depicting a world map with the equator. It has my name on it recording my crossing of the line today; a welcome goodwill gesture. I read my book about the Victorian tourists and turn in at 10.30pm. I don't sleep well and have a bad dream featuring women I worked with at Rio Tinto during my disagreeable last year of full-time employment. Very strange; what subconscious trigger made that pop up while I am on the best jolly of my life?

Thursday 19 January

At Sea. Noon position 6S 1W

I wake at 5am then doze to 6am and get up at 6.15am. With my laundry back and so many clean shirts I realise I probably brought too many: I had provided for a shirt a day and not doing laundry. I go up on the Observation deck. It is 6.40am and just becoming light. The sky is cloudy with puffy black rain clouds. The deck is wet from the rain. On the sundeck the crews are again hosing down an already spotless expanse of planking.

Wherever you go on the ship all day, crews are cleaning, powerwashing, painting. Men wearing the safety harness required for working at heights wash and polish the glass roof over the pool. There is often the smell of fresh varnish inside and outside the ship. I get a coffee and sit at a table near Dennis. He is still snuffling. I say it must be a sinus problem if it comes and goes. If it persists he will be like that until Australia. He says on his one other cruise on the *QM2* he got an ear infection and treatment cost £300, though he did get it back from insurance.

We talk about the Union Castle ships between England and Cape Town. I tell him in 1971 S and I opted to fly on the new Vickers VC10 jet to South Africa after we got married although we were offered a passage by sea. Now I'm making good on what I missed then by sailing into Table Bay from England. It turns out Dennis knows the VC10s and flew aboard them as a flight attendant. He suggests maybe he was on our flight as he was working in 1971.

For breakfast I have paw-paw followed by an omelette and smoked fish on bread. On the way out I take a peach and eat it while I watch the TV screens. The *Costa Concordia* seems to have dropped down the news agenda. We are already 3deg S. The weather is breezy but not cold. It is not that pleasant on deck. Dennis said previously he is surprised it is not warmer on the equator. I think it is the wind, it blows constantly.

At home in Farnham I have a book of news photographs from the *Cape Argus* from the 1970s and 1980s. Among them is a dramatic aerial shot of the *Queen Elizabeth 2* at anchor outside Cape Town with a backdrop of black clouds and Lion's Head. The caption reads: "*The QE2 rides at anchor in windy, white-flecked Table Bay early in the morning as Cape Town glowers under a black south-easter. Docking of the world's tallest and costliest liner was delayed by the gale-force south-easterly wind. 29.1.1975."* That's 37 years ago almost to the day. Later I will describe how the *QM2* was similarly delayed by the Cape south-easter, this time from leaving Cape Town.

I thought the picture might be of interest to somebody on the *QM2* so I had the spread photocopied at a print shop. I thought today is a good time to give it to one of the officers on the bridge. I see them coming and going on Deck 12. As I step into the lobby there is the Chief Engineer Brian Wattling coming out. I recognise him from his biography in the *Daily Programme*. He comes from Brighton.

We have a quick introductory chat and I give him my *QE2* picture saying it may be of interest to the officers on the bridge. He says thanks and adds he will give it to the Commodore as well. He says the *QM2* will not get stuck outside if there is a gale blowing because her propulsion system makes her very manoeuvrable with its front side thrusters and swivelling engine pods that serve as both propeller and rudder. He says the *QE2*'s old technology made it quite a cumbersome ship to manoeuvre. He returns to the bridge with my piece of paper.

At 10am the ship's company start another safety exercise that does not involve us passengers. We are the precious cargo being protected and hear lots of announcements that apply only to the crew.

The noon navigational announcement says we are at six degrees south of the equator, 850 miles due west of the mouth of the Congo River and 610 miles from the Island of St Helena to the west (where Napoleon was imprisoned after his defeat at Waterloo). We have travelled another 507 miles since noon yesterday and have 1,300 miles to Walvis Bay. The water and sea temperatures have parted company, with the sea cooler at 24C and the air still at 27C.

We have a strong south-easterly wind which makes walking on deck uncomfortable. I go down to lunch at the King's Court and have a salad with cold meat. I am just in time for Hugh Hudson's next show *Greystoke the Legend of Tarzan* in the Illuminations theatre. Hollywood made Tarzan famous by developing the idea of a jungle man as lord of the apes, the hero in a series of adventures. This movie is faithful to the original Edgar Rice Burroughs story; from the parents, Lord and Lady Greystoke, being shipwrecked off West Africa with their baby and how the parents die and the baby is befriended by the apes and brought up by them. It is the same idea as Mowgli in Kipling's *Jungle Book*.

Tarzan grows to adulthood, is then rescued by a botanist exploring in West Africa, and is brought back to Scotland to claim his inheritance, the Greystoke estate and its wealth. He has trouble fitting in, of course. He goes to the Natural History Museum in London to open a new wing he has funded and finds one of the family of apes who brought him up being kept in a cage. He literally goes ape again, hooting and rapping his knuckles on the ground, ending up in a tree in Hyde Park in his Victorian suit with his "kindred" ape. He decides to return to the jungle where he was brought up. The production (1984) seems ponderous and too long. I do not enjoy it much, except for the interesting idea that a human can genuinely be part of a sub-human group and communicate emotions with them in sounds and gestures.

I go down to the Purser's office where you can line up to ask questions of the staff at the counter. Out of interest I want to check what my bill amounts to. It turns out to be $518, which is about £330, so not bad and definitely below budget. I get out for a much needed walk on deck. The morning cloud has gone and it is a hot afternoon with a clear sky, blue sea and visibility clear to the horizon. The water is calm, but at the top of the ship the south-east wind is still strong.

I go down and read beside the pool and then have a swim before going in to change for dinner. It is semi-formal so quite easy and comfortable. I make it down to the Chartroom bar at 20 minutes before dinner time and the redoubtable Lena mixes me a Martini without so much as asking what I want. She also provides me with a special plate of warm canapes which are normally walked round by a server from table to table. Later on when I sign for my drink I want to give her a token of thanks for her service by adding a tip to the automatic 15 per cent, thinking she will get the extra. But no, she says it is shared by all the bar staff, whereas the servers keep any extra tips they get for themselves.

Dinner is convivial and fun. We seem to get on well and have a good laugh, so much so that people at other tables turn and look. I tell the story of *Greystoke* and give an impression of the monkey sounds Tarzan makes to communicate (whoo-whoo) which brings loud laughter. They say I should sign up for the talent contest as a mimic.

I have delicious barramundi, an Australian fish that must have clocked up some food miles to get on our plates in the South Atlantic. Some of the others have lamb shank off the bone which looks meaty and tender. Margaret gets a large portion and Joe next to her a smaller portion, and he is the big guy. You can see him looking envious. This also happened a few nights ago when beef was served and Margaret got more and Joe less. I join Joe in joking about the discrepancy and Roger pipes up: "It's probably because Margaret is going on the whole voyage and you are the freeloader." I think this is very rude and say so, but Joe, ever the polite Canadian, laughingly brushes it off by saying that Margaret deserves the bigger portions more than he does. Roger says he's sorry, he will wash his mouth out.

After dinner, at about 8.30pm there is a good jazz trio playing in the Chartroom and couples are coming in to have a cocktail and enjoy the music. I was there before the crowds came so I have a good spot and enjoy a few whiskies. The trouble is when you are alone, if you get up to go to the toilet you come back and you have lost your place so have to start again elsewhere. I have fun chatting to people at the bar until about 11.30pm and decide to call it a night. When I get back to my cabin I realise we have to turn our clocks forward again so it is actually 12.30am. So I finally go off to sleep at about 1am.

Friday 20 January

At Sea. Noon position 12S 3E

Late night or not, I am awake at 6am and wait to get up at about 6.30am. I shave and dress and go to the Observation deck to see the weather but it is closed with a sign saying "High Winds". I could feel the ship's movement when I was in bed. But when I get down to Deck 7 for coffee and look out as the dawn breaks, the sea is quite flat and the wind not that strong on this level of the ship.

I have discovered the coffee tastes more like coffee if you use the milk called half and half – cream and milk. The milk jugs are always full and you never get a situation where they are out of something you want. They have full cream, skim and semi-skimmed milk as well as half and half, in grey jugs with labels. It is 7am and I am too late for Dennis and the whole place is rather empty for that time of the morning. I take the opportunity to ask the chef at the buffet to cook me fried eggs. They are far from fresh judging by the big spread of white but it is okay. I decide I'd better skip lunch except for fruit.

The main agenda item today is a showing of the film *Rupture* at 3pm. The blurb in the *Daily Programme* says: "Maryam d'Abo had a brain rupture three years ago and almost died. She lived to tell this inspiring story of her suffering and the suffering of many others. The film shows a life affirming journey and gives an understanding to help those and the families that have been afflicted by or witnessed this frightening occurrence, ending ultimately with hope and affirmation. A powerful and moving film, and a very personal one for Maryam and her husband Hugh, they will introduce this special screening and answer questions from the audience at its conclusion. Film duration 70 minutes."

I spend the morning enjoying the book about Continental travel by the British and go out on deck a lot to see if I can see any flying fish. Carol from Woking says they saw masses of them yesterday from their balcony. Harold Nicolson described flying fish as being like "small tin model aeroplanes" that awkwardly flit rather than fly. The noon Navigation announcement says we are 12 degrees south of the equator, have just crossed the Greenwich meridian into the eastern hemisphere and are 570 miles west of Benguela in Angola.

The Commodore reminds us that we are sailing against the cold Benguela current. It comes north from Antarctica up the west coast and is responsible for South Africa's abundant west coast fishery. With a cold sea and the beating of the south east wind it is not too hot, though the sun has taken on the harsh glare of the south. I'm putting on sunscreen and wearing a hat. We are in very deep water, with more than 18,000ft beneath our hull. We have covered 518 miles since yesterday noon, so we are keeping up a steady pace of 500 miles a day, with 913 miles to Walvis Bay.

I have a half sandwich and a peach for lunch and listen to the VIBZ steel band playing on the stern deck among the rich and ancient Princess Grillers. I go down to Illuminations for the 3pm movie about the brain haemorrhage. The survivor, Maryam d'Abo, is trying to make sense of what happened to her. She is emotional during her introduction as if talking about it still brings back the pain and fright.

The movie has Maryam telling her story to camera, sometimes speaking over dreamy shots of G F Watts's statue of *Energy* in Kensington Gardens, interspersed with footage and interviews with neurosurgeons describing the wonders of the brain, how it works and what happens when it is injured. Not even the surgeons can fathom how a merely physical organ, complex and miraculous as it is, can make us into spiritual beings and give us the self awareness and concept of past, present and future, which no other living creature possesses. The rest of the 70 minute film is on victims of other brain injuries and their stories, all different and unique, but it muddles the main focus which is about spontaneous, sudden bleeds on the brain.

Maryam's husband Hugh Hudson rightly described these in the Q&A as ticking time bombs that all of us have in our heads. The feature is worth watching but goes on too long. None of the cases depicted match up with what S went through with her crushing weight loss, but they all involve a great deal of pain and distress, with deep depression, self bereavement and anger. In the Q&A session people in the audience tell of the circumstances of brain injured people they know about and an American hopes if it will be shown on TV in her country. I am not inclined to speak about the ordeal I shared with my wife, it is between ourselves.

However, afterwards I go down and ask for Maryam's email address, explaining that my wife is a survivor and when she sees the film on the BBC she may want to contact her. I take the chance to give a brief account of S's story, but standing on the stage looking down Maryam is affected by the ship's movements and you can see she is uncomfortable and not able to take it in. She scrawls out her email address for me.

Back in my cabin I shower and change into my formal suit for the last time of the voyage. Tonight is African Ball night. Down at dinner we discuss accommodation on the ship and the points you earn in the loyalty scheme for the status of the cabin and the length of voyage. Roger and Carol, who are going all the way to Australia then circumnavigating the continent, are up there with a gold rating. I am silver which is bottom, and the top one is diamond. Each level confers privileges, the one most useful sounding is four hours of free internet time in the ship's computer room, Connexions.

Roger and Carol have a cabin they specially chose in the middle of the ship close to the waterline on Deck 5. They are obviously seasoned cruise people. They say this part of the ship moves the least – in the middle and low down. I think to myself I'd rather feel the movement swaying up top and be close to the front, as I am. However, Carol has seen a lot of flying fish and a school of dolphins from far off, which you can see better near the waterline. I have looked in vain from the decks but Carol says I would probably not see them from a high angle.

I ask Joe, who has contact with the working part of the ship, about where the crew go when they are off duty. I am thinking not so much of the seamen, but the servers, entertainers and stewards. I discover there is another dimension behind the scenes, in parts of the ship passengers don't know about. The crews sleep and eat and pass their time when off duty in the invisible innards of the ship located mainly on Deck 1 and below, and elsewhere behind doors marked "No Entry" or "Crew Passageway". They make up a separate class only visible when required. It reminds me of one of those Russian dolls of different sizes that all fit inside one another; worlds within worlds, giving the illusion of one.

In their world, the crew have their own stainless steel buffet area for meals and a bar and recreation rooms. When off duty, and it probably isn't much down time, they are absolutely forbidden from entering the guest areas on pain of instant dismissal. Joe said he asked a crew member to give him a haircut in his cabin (he is in a no-go area for crew) and the person was very nervous about coming to him and had to be quick. The crew have access to their own outdoor deck which is a raised area around the base of the rear secondary funnels not accessible to passengers.

It seems crew conditions have improved somewhat over the years. In the travel book *English Journey* written in 1934, J B Priestley chatted to a ship's steward at a bus stop in Southampton, who told him working aboard the passenger liners was a rotten life. "*Bad quarters. Working all hours. And no proper food and nowhere to eat it. If you're a steward, you've got to stand up and snatch a bite when you can. Even with the tips it's no good. I've had enough of it, sir, I can tell you.*" Priestley, who sailed on the liners, correctly comments: *Most of us would be willing to give up a little space in the ship and a few items from the menu if we knew that the people waiting upon us were being allowed to lead a civilized life.* Happily, this has come to pass.

I hear Roger and Carol have volunteered to take part in the Guest Talent Show tomorrow afternoon; I imagine this staunchly British suburban couple are going to sing a song from the Vera Lynn repertoire. After dinner I go to the Royal Court Theatre for the headline show of the night, *Apassionata*, featuring the Royal Cunard Singers and Dancers.

It is a very slickly produced variety show with different themes. There are Spanish costumes and salsa; Cossack dancing that is incredibly energetic and hard to do, leaping about from a squatting position; and music from the dawn of pop, the 1950s with the full skirts and bobby socks. The staging is polished, with revolving mirrors through which the dancers come and go, backed by a full live orchestra behind the stage. I enjoy the show and am impressed by the amazing speed of costume changes.

There are six couples and at the end of a sequence they vanish and two come on and start the next song and dance and are joined within minutes by the rest of the troupe who have all been magically transformed into the next theme, sometimes even with different hairstyles for the girls. My thoughts turn to the logistics of this. They have a limited number of cast members so the team have to work hard and fill multiple roles. What an opportunity for the all-rounder.

One sequence has an entrance of performers coming up on a section of stage raised from a lower level. There can't be many cruise ships with such sophisticated staging. And all these performers and production people live out of sight of us passengers and magically appear in their theatrical costumes for our entertainment. At the final curtain, the master of ceremonies proudly introduces them one by one, by name and country of origin as they take a bow; singers and dancers from all over the world – young, energetic and making a name for themselves with a gig on the *QM2*.

They do the 45 minute show all over again for the late crowd at 10.45pm. That's show business.

Saturday 21 January

At Sea. Noon position 18S 9E

I awake at 6.15am and follow my usual route out of the ship at the front, along the deck to halfway along the hull, then down the internal stairs to have coffee with Dennis, followed by a sitdown breakfast in the Britannia restaurant. I sit with a lady from Wales whose husband is on board with her. She exclaims with happiness how wonderful it is "to have lovely fresh towels each day, not to have to think of meals, or shopping, or laundry and be quite free to enjoy yourself". Quite so.

We are joined by a couple from Midhurst, West Sussex, which is not far south of Farnham. The lady's mother has just died in England since they left so they are cutting short a two week holiday at the Cape and flying home for the funeral. They were able to organise flights from the ship's computer room. They seem surprisingly composed. On the other side of me is a couple I met at lunch one day. He worked in Montreal with Seagrams. They live in west Scotland and the lady complains of the constant rain there. I eat a pink grapefruit half, and a plain omelette with American bacon and a British sausage. The man from Seagrams compliments me on being able to eat the bacon with a knife and fork; he says it is so crispy he can't cut it without shattering it all over the table, so he eats it with his fingers.

In my cabin I watch a TV programme on the Union Castle ships repeated on a loop. The ship interiors on the grainy film look so old fashioned, but those were the days. Perhaps it was just as well I waited for the more modern era to make my voyage to Cape Town. However, our voyage is now feeling rather drawn out, not having seen land for six days. Leo told me at dinner last night he overheard a lady on deck tell her husband: "This is lovely but I wish we could arrive." But there are always new events coming up and the next stage to look forward to. The big ship with all its fine spaces has become a familiar place. I love looking at the ocean and watching the waves made by the ship butting the breakers made by the wind, throwing white water like lacy tablecloths away to the side against the blue surface.

And as we heard from the lady from Wales at breakfast, it is bliss to be without immediate obligations; to have no diary; to be able to either choose an activity from the programme or say no thanks, without any social or family consequences. For example, the most difficult and arduous tasks I have set for myself today are to watch football in the pub with a few beers and catch the Guest Talent Show, if I remember.

The sea today is a deep aquamarine and it is quite calm except near the ship where the water is disturbed. The water is a cold 21 degrees and the air temperature 23C, made chillier by the constant south-easterly wind into which we are sailing. These are the trade winds that fuelled ocean commerce for centuries before the age of steam. At noon we are only 160 miles from the coast of Africa, near Cape Fria in northern Namibia. We have covered 513 miles in the last 24 hours and 3,455 miles since we left Tenerife. Beneath the ship is 14,000ft of water so we are not yet over the continental shelf that juts out from Africa.

I spend much of the morning reading, first on the shady side of the ship on a deckchair facing the sea; but I feel the cold from the wind and go indoors to the poolside on Deck 12. The area has the sliding roof closed so the sun warms. Most people you see when you are out and about are on the loungers lying back and reading. It's cabin or balcony, organised activity or bar and buffet, otherwise passengers are lolling on deck, not unlike a colony of sunning walruses when you survey them *en masse* on the expanse of the sundeck.

They read novels identifiable as having come out of the ship's library, and a surprisingly large number have the Kindle readers, which have the added advantage of not having pages to flap in the wind. I notice some people have the print size turned up pretty high, perhaps so they don't have to wear glasses. For lunch I have a sandwich and a peach. Back on the sundeck I succumb to the temptation of a hot dog. I had checked there was a table I could sit at before going into the sundeck buffet, but when I come out, the tables are all taken and there is no place to join anyone. Luckily there is a lone unoccupied chair against a bulkhead in the shade so I park myself there.

I go to the Golden Lion pub where all the gents are waiting for the satellite feed to bring them a Football Feast. This Saturday there are three games scheduled, lasting from 2.30 to 8.30pm, all live from the UK. I watch the first from Norwich where the locals hold Chelsea to a 0-0 draw. I go to my cabin early to get ready so that I can see the Guest Talent Show at 5pm and be ready for dinner at 6pm.

I arrive late in the Queen's Room and find I have missed Roger and Carol's contribution. There is a rhyme being recited by an elderly American woman, then a toe-curling Jimmy Durante imitation, a Scotsman playing the bagpipes not very well, a South African playing the piano not very well, and a very British gent of the old school doing a rope trick. I wander off to the lobby outside the ballroom and admire the beautiful scale model of the QM2 in a glass case. From my knowledge of the ship, it is accurate to the last detail. I notice the propellers face forward like an aircraft so they pull the ship instead of pushing it.

At dinner, Margaret has brought her bottle of Pol Aker sparkling wine from her cabin. She hasn't thought to chill it although she would have had an ice bucket in her room plus a minibar cold space. The wine steward puts it in a neighbouring table's ice bucket stand and we have to wait for a drink until later. It turns out that Roger and Carol's participation in the Guest Talent Show was not anything like I imagined. They were not singing a duet from Vera Lynn but had joined a choir of 80 who opened the show. Even I could have done that.

Tomorrow we spend the day in the port of Walvis Bay (Whale Bay). People ask me about Namibia and I tell them what I know. Joe says he is afraid of this part of the world: he associates it always with violence and injustice. But he is going ashore with Leo to have a look. I can't imagine there is much to see except the lagoon with flamingoes and a mountain of sand in the desert called Dune 7. I remember it from when I was there with a film crew making videos for Rio Tinto at the Rössing Uranium mine in 2005.

I tell them that Namibia has a mining industry, especially uranium. Carol gives a shudder and says she hopes it is not dangerous. I explain that the concentration of uranium in the ore at Rössing is only 0.03 per cent and is harmless in the form in which it is mined. It is radioactive only once processed and concentrated. It then goes to the US or elsewhere for further processing into fuel rods for electric power stations. I add that China is building more than 40 new nuclear power stations and the Fukushima accident, far from showing the dangers of nuclear power, showed that nothing too bad can happen even when the plant is knocked out. Roger, who up to this point has been listening without saying anything, backs me up. He agrees that the greatest nuclear power danger – the disposal of spent fuel rods – can also be overcome. Apparently Roger was a health and safety officer in Britain's North Sea oil fields.

The excursions advertised for Walvis Bay include looking at desert plants at a "moon landscape", a seal and dolphin cruise (which Margaret is going on), a tour of the neighbouring town of Swakopmund with its German architecture, and a visit to a township. I am asked to explain how I came by my local knowledge.

I remember visiting Walvis Bay when it was a military base in the 1970s. I was Defence Correspondent of *The Star* in Johannesburg and my new wife from England was working at an x-ray practice in Jeppe Street. I was in a group of reporters given a tour by the South African military, which had a base in the South African owned harbour enclave of Walvis Bay to counter insurgency from Angola on the northern border of what at the time was called South West Africa, now Namibia. Because South Africa followed a policy of racial segregation the international community was questioning its right to administer South West Africa.

I don't remember much of the visit but I do recall I borrowed S's best small suitcase for the trip. It was placed in the underside luggage compartment of the military bus to the airport, next to the exhaust pipe which became so hot it scorched a hole in the case. It could have caught fire. Back home in Johannesburg, S was not best pleased as the suitcase had to be discarded.

These tales lead to Margaret asking how I met my wife. I tell my story, then Margaret relates how she met her husband – involving motorbikes and the practice of meeting to kick tyres and take photographs at a roadside café – and then Roger and Carol have a turn. They met by chance when Roger, in a state of student homelessness, was invited to share a flat with his mates. One night the boys upstairs were making such a noise that Carol, who lived below and had been knocking on her ceiling with a squash racket, came up to tell them to be quiet.

Roger was sent down next day to apologise and the rest, as they say, is history. I point out that our stories show that the weight of fortune hangs on a thread. When I first asked S out on a date she couldn't do Saturday night, nor Friday, and no, not Thursday either. I was about to hang up the phone, when a small voice piped up that she was free that night, Wednesday. If she hadn't said anything, our lives would have taken quite different directions.

After dinner I go into the Golden Lion pub for more football. I sit there a short while and feel too full to drink beer. I had chicken livers and onion with a poached egg on toast as a starter, and rib of beef for the main followed by cheesecake. I decide I had better have a walk so go up to the sundeck. I am in time to watch the sunset from the highest viewpoint in the middle of the ship. It is a beautiful scene, the sea spreading dark and gold in all directions to the horizon, which is only 13 miles away, though it looks much further.

I soon feel better and go down to the football. There is an open space at the bar in front of the television but no stool. I have to be close because the satellite picture is not sharp and I can't see clearly from a distance. It is hard even to read the scoreline and the time elapsed. I watch the second half of the last game, Bolton Wanderers v Liverpool. Against expectations, Bolton win. It is an absorbing game. Each Brit in the room seems to have a favourite team. They are very partisan, football being a tribal thing. I like to watch any high level sport just for the spectacle and the skill on display without much caring who wins, though I tend to back the underdogs. I tuck into gin and bitter lemon during the game. My total bill must be approaching $650. I go up to bed and read.

Hugh ready for the first formal night on board the QM2.

Sunny climes - the market garden slopes of Madeira.

In port - the QM2 shares the dock in Madeira
with a Canadian frigate, HMCS Vancouver.

Spanish outpost in the North Atlantic,
the port of Santa Cruz de Tenerife.

Tropic days - spectacular cloud formations loom over
a placid sea as the QM2 ploughs across the equator.

Big day - while Table Mountain was obscured for arrival
in Cape Town it was still a magical morning.

Dominant and superb - Table Mountain
from the QM2 in Table Bay.

Sailaway - The QM2 leaves Cape Town's Duncan Dock at
6am on 27 January, her departure delayed 12 hours by a gale.

Chapter 4

Benguela

Sunday 22 January

Walvis Bay, Namibia

I wake up in the dark as usual (no windows) and check my clock. It is 5.45am and I get up as I want to see the approach into Walvis Bay. I pull on my jeans and put my windbreaker jacket over my pyjama top and put on shoes without socks. The Observation deck one level below me is open after being shut for two days due to strong winds. I step out and it is just getting light. There is a strong land smell of fish. The sky is grey and overcast and the wind is chilly.

I can see a row of yellow lights on my left and another row of whiter lights on my right. There are irregular bits of light straight ahead. The ship is moving quite rapidly judging by the white water alongside but not as fast as on the open sea. I work out that the yellow lights on the port side must be Swakopmund and the lights on the starboard side Walvis Bay, with ships at anchor ahead. There are couples with me speaking German and craning their necks to see down the port side of the ship.

The Observation deck juts out like the bridge so looking backwards you can see what's going on alongside. In the half light there is an open vessel the size of a tug close by, keeping up with the *QM2*, and another smaller speedboat outside of that. The tugsize vessel comes close and locks itself against the ship. It does not attach itself with a line but skillfully travels alongside at the same speed as the *QM2*, pressing against the big ship's side. Neither vessel slackens pace; they continue to make white water as about 20 figures in high visibility red lifejackets are seen boarding the liner one by one from the open vessel. Then a person in whites and gold braid without a lifejacket boards the ship and the small vessel veers away. It picks up speed with the speedboat beside it, overtakes the *QM2* and heads for shore. This is the group of immigration officers come to check us for entry into Namibia.

As the dawn brightens I see we are heading into a neat lane of marker buoys, green on the starboard side of the ship, red on the port side. As we approach the lane appears to be too narrow, but once between the marker buoys there is enough space. We are heading direct for two bright navigation lights, green and red, which mark the dock. The shore comes closer as the light improves. The shore is a huddle of nondescript roofs and dock cranes, with a line of brown, sandy hills behind. Even Tenerife looks much grander. Through my binoculars I look for people who may be out to greet the biggest cruise ship ever to visit Walvis Bay. There are a few dockworkers in hard hats and overalls but only one small group of civilians with cameras. They wave.

The ship's bow comes up close to the dock at a 90 degree angle. It seems only yards away from the concrete, then using its fore and aft swivel propellers it slowly turns the bows to port so that the ship is like a door closing on the length of the dock with the bows as the hinge-fulcrum. It is very neatly done, avoiding a green marker buoy behind us which I thought looked too close.

I watch the crews tying up the ship. A seaman on the *QM2* throws a heavy object attached to a light line which lands on the dock and is picked up by the docking crew. They tug this in as the ship gets closer and the light line pulls the heavy hawsers with it so that the looped ends can be draped round the bollard on the dock. Then the lines are tightened from within the ship as she is tied fast and can't move. They put a concave circular disc on the hawser at the dockside so that no rodents can run along the rope and into the ship.

This is a working port, with rail lines set into the concrete dock surface and huge mobile cranes that unload containers. There are hundreds of containers stacked along the dock with wheeled hydraulic loaders roaring about to move them. The massive cranes are also mobile on rubber tyres with a hydraulic leg at each corner to provide stability for heavy lifting. They have all been moved away and cordoned off with red-striped warning tape.

Cunard set up their spotless white English marquees at the foot of the two gangways with the *Queen Mary 2* banners along the railings. A special *QM2* rug is placed at the entrance and safety nets are secured beneath the gangway. British high standards contrast with the bleak desert landscape and the industrial grit of a working port in its Sunday best. Onlookers arrive taking pictures, pointing and discussing. It must be the talk of the town. I have breakfast in the King's Court: omelette and smoked fish, toast and orange juice.

At 9am, the time specified for people on Deck 12, I go down to the Queen's Room where we are to have immigration procedures, even for those not planning to go ashore like myself. The immigration officers wear informal red polo shirts with the Namibian coat of arms on one side and an AIDS symbol, the white crossed ribbon, on the other with the words "We Care". I imagined long queues but there are none. Tables draped with white linen are set out on the ballroom floor and the immigration officers are numerous enough to have time to chat with one another.

I go to a table and the officer goes through my passport page by page with great interest. He says with some surprise "You have been here before". I said I visited Rössing but he makes no comment. I tell him I am not going ashore. I am checked into Namibia and then immediately checked out again. He stamps both my yellow card I have filled in for entry and my white card for exit, keeps them both, stamps my passport for a one day visit and next to it an exit stamp, and I am on my way. It is a dry run for disembarkation in Cape Town where immigration officers will also be coming aboard to process visitors.

It is a quiet day with a lot of people away and the *QM2* is suddenly almost a ghost ship. I can go about without seeing many people, taking pictures of the public spaces and going on deck to take more pictures of the flat roofs of Walvis Bay and the desert behind. Looking down on the dockside all the people going and coming are passengers, with little sign of any locals taking an interest.

Crews are unloading mattresses from an opening in the ship at dockside level using forklift trucks. I remember that several decks had their mattresses changed for new during the voyage. I presume the old mattresses are being donated by Cunard to a charity in Namibia which is a heart-warming idea, instead of taking them home to a British landfill. The mattresses are stacked on a lorry, which takes about 100 of them and comes back later for more.

A forklift is also loading bales of recyclables and garbage into dumpsters that are taken away by a truck. Leo suddenly joins me at the rail. He and Joe were ashore for a short while, now they are back. There was nothing to see and most stores were closed. Shops that were open were shutting at 1pm. They went to see a supermarket (I spotted Pick 'n Pay through my binoculars earlier) and most of the people in there were also curious tourists.

The only interesting place was the Seafarers' Club which they visited. It had a shop with local goods, but most of the stock was factory made in China. Crew members from the *QM2*, including the entertainers who dance and sing, were availing themselves of a day off at the bar.

I have a peach for lunch and go to see more football in the Golden Lion. I have a few beers while watching Manchester City v Tottenham Hotspur, a good match-up as they are both battling for top spot in the league. City are two goals ahead when Spurs catch up and level the scores, only to lose in extra time when City score their third goal. I feel vaguely guilty sitting here doing what I would have done at home when it is hot and sunny outside and I could be looking around Walvis Bay. It is a relief when we sail at 5pm in bright sunshine.

At dinner I hear that Margaret had a successful Seal and Dolphin Watching excursion, seeing the genuine article. A seal jumped into the boat when offered a bucket of fish, but apparently the tour guide knows the seal and it is half tame. Then they went to see wild seals on a beach further on. Roger and Carol are disappointed by Dune 7, a pile of sand, and also with the town of Swakopmund, which they found uninteresting and closed up.

One thing they did enjoy was a private museum with free entry full of curiosities like stuffed baboons, birds and a leopard. They took pictures of these to show their grandchildren. It sounds as if Walvis Bay needs to wake up to the economic opportunity of having on their doorstep more than 1,000 visitors with money to spend when a major cruise ship is in port.

At dinner I sit next to Leo and we have a one-on-one about the circumstances of my leaving South Africa. I tell him we wanted to move away and the choice was Canada or England, which we decided against because it had economic problems. Canada seemed to offer more opportunity, but once there we struggled to settle down in a society that was much more unfamiliar than we had expected. After landing a temporary summer job as a reporter in my first week in Vancouver, I moved on to writing for a public relations agency for C$25 an hour, before accepting a low level salary for my first corporate job because I was fairly desperate. It was eight years and another job before I felt I was being fairly treated. However, Canada and my first corporate job got me started on a new and interesting career in the mining sector, which would have been an unlikely choice in England, and the industry expertise I gained in Canada helped make me a success in London.

Nevertheless, maybe going to England in the first place might have been a better bet. At least we would have been in familiar territory, making it easier to settle and find a job. More importantly, we would have kept our family together. The children would have become British in outlook and education like their mother. Now we are culturally different and spread around. We lose out on each other's company, missing the news and the secondary details of daily life that bind families together. Occasional phone calls and emails aren't the same as frequent face time.

At the end of the meal, Alex the steward presents us each with a folder of our complete dinner menus with a handwritten note on each package saying it was a pleasure serving us and she and her colleague Arnold hope we were well pleased. I remember from the New York voyage this is the way of signalling that they expect a cash gratuity. As mentioned, Cunard debit your account with $11 a day to cover gratuities to stewards. Additionally, we pay 15 per cent on every bar purchase. Anyway, I decide the right thing to do is to give banknotes to the Britannia stewards as well as Dong my stateroom steward. A folder in the cabin contains envelopes so I put English banknotes in one for Alex and Arnold and South African notes in another for Dong, and write thank you messages.

We are back at cruising speed heading south to Cape Town; now we are properly into the southern summer. The day is longer and the sun out until 7.45pm. I spend some of the evening reading information about disembarkation. I exchange texts with my sister Val who says she will be on the dockside to meet the QM2 at 6am on Tuesday and my room is ready. I think there might be quite a wait for her as the information says the guests going on Cape Town excursions get priority to disembark and I might be off only about 9.30am.

My last set of laundry is returned and I carefully fold the beautifully laundered shirts for packing. I go to bed and read my book. I can't get to sleep, not because there is anything on my mind but I just don't feel sleepy. The ship moves a lot, much more than at any other time on the voyage, as we sail into the teeth of a south-easterly wind. The cabin fittings creak now and then, there are slight vibrations, and you occasionally feel pressure on your body as the ship moves from side to side. We're afloat all right.

Monday 23 January

At Sea. Noon position 28S 13E

I was up at 2.20am and 4.10am and did not go into a deep sleep all night as I have been doing before. Lying awake waiting for the alarm to go off at 6.10am I resolve to change my plan for disembarkation. I imagine Val will be there from before 6am tomorrow so I should not keep her waiting. And there should be no consideration of trying to hang on to the lovely shipboard life for a few more hours because this is my last full day and by tonight it is over.

I had planned to pack before dinner tonight and leave my big case outside my door for the porters to take overnight. You then pick it up in a tent on the dock when you disembark in the morning; in my instance it would have been about 9.30am. There was an offer in the information package of Self Help Disembarkation. You carry all your own bags as there are no porters and you have to go early, before everybody else.

This means being in the Queen's Room for the immigration clearance by 6.45am and departure at or soon after 7am. I go down to the Purser's office on my way to Deck 7 for coffee. I tell the young man I want to join the early birds, he puts it in the computer and gives me a special card to show my status, confirms the timings and I am away.

Dennis is eating his breakfast and I have coffee. I had tried going on deck at the front of the ship as usual but the doors were barred with the sign "Closed High Winds". Seeing out, the sun is well up. It had risen at 7am. It confirmed to me I had done the right thing organising to leave the ship early. For Val, 6am at the dockside is probably no great hardship as it would be getting light, so my leaving the ship early will fit into her routine.

Dennis discusses the Walvis Bay experience which he found disappointing. The shuttle buses were a nightmare as people boarded and got off so slowly there were long waits. He gave up and started walking along the route he could see the buses followed. On street corners people asked him for money and there was nothing of interest to see. He went past the Seafarers' Club but did not go in. So he was back on board within an hour and a bit. He wonders what the passenger consensus will be about Walvis Bay and whether Cunard will come again. On the other hand they need the stop because Tenerife to Walvis Bay is already the longest time at sea (seven days) of any leg of the voyage. Direct to Cape Town would be eight days. Maybe they should call somewhere in West Africa.

I go to my cabin, put out the envelope for Dong and get ready to go to the first activity of the day, Ambassador Howard Walker speaking about South Africa as a regional power. He wears what South Africans call a "safari suit" – matching long khaki trousers and open neck short sleeve top like a jacket, worn with a cravat. He was US Ambassador to South Africa starting in 1980, just when I left for Canada, but before that he was second in charge, so must have overlapped with my spell as political correspondent of *The Star*.

He obviously loves South Africa, has many personal friends there from his tour of duty, and has basically stayed on as he says he has an apartment in Bantry Bay, an upmarket suburb on the Atlantic coast of Cape Town. He and his wife are on their way for an annual three month stay during the northern winter. He calls himself a snow bird. At the end of his talk I introduce myself. He looks at me and asks jokingly if I am William Hague (the bald-headed British Foreign Secretary). I tell him I left South Africa when he started as Ambassador. A "scholarship" to tour the US for familiarisation that was meant for me as political correspondent went to my successor, Peter Sullivan, who came to see us in Vancouver in 1981. I ask if he knows Jim Carragher who was my contact at the US Embassy and he says yes, he is a close friend of his. Jim is still in service at the State Department in Washington.

In his talk he has interesting insights into the way South Africa is going, generally positive. The country's transition from minority rule to a full democracy surprised foreign observers like him who expected it to be accompanied by more strife and bloodshed than actually occurred. He says the transition should serve as a model for other divided communities in the world. South Africa earned the moral high ground in the eyes of the world, but now this is being eroded by actions that give priority to the national interest.

For instance it does not support the people of Zimbabwe against the dictator Mugabe, nor the people of Burma against the ruling generals. Yet South Africa is the most powerful economic and military force in Africa south of the Sahara. It has a growing middle class that doubles in number every three years. It is a functioning democracy with a wide choice for voters, and a free press. People who left South Africa are coming back to start businesses, he says. There are elements who want the country to go in a more socialist direction to help the underprivileged, but the key players in setting economic policy want to keep the capitalist economy. Bond issues (the way governments borrow money) have been taken up by world markets more rapidly than, say, bonds offered by Italy and Portugal. He skates over the issues of crime and security and the weakness of the rand since the end of apartheid despite the growth of the economy.

Outside on deck the wind is still strong south-easterly and the waves are bursting up against the starboard side. It is unpleasant in the wind so I watch the waves breaking on the ship from a seat by the window on Deck 3 outside the lecture theatre. I go to the shop to buy Val and Stephen *QM2* souvenir mugs. Many others have caught the shopping bug on the last day at sea before Cape Town.

I text Val that I am due to get off at 7am tomorrow. Immediately after, Sod's Law (Murphy's Law in Canada) strikes again. In the Commodore's noon announcement, he says the Cape Town port authorities have asked the *QM2* to dock after 8am to allow for a shift change of pilotage and dock personnel. The timing will alter my disembarkation plans.

The Commodore reports that we are 25 miles west of the African coast near the Namibia-South Africa border at Oranjemund, the mouth of the Orange River. This is 338 miles from Walvis Bay with 383 miles to run to Table Bay. We have crossed the Tropic of Capricorn into the southern temperate zone. The forecast for Cape Town tomorrow is partly cloudy, a high of 26C with a fresh south-easter.

I have a proper lunch of beef bourguignon, rice and broccoli at the King's Court buffet, then go to the Royal Court theatre for a piano recital by the sublime Allan Schiller. He has a shock of grey hair and wears heavy dark rimmed glasses like Arthur Miller. He must be in his late 50s or early 60s. He takes the microphone for his introduction and says this is his last concert on the *QM2* as he is getting off in Cape Town tomorrow.

"As much as I have enjoyed the voyage I will be glad to get home to my dear wife who is missing me. I miss the weather," he adds, tongue in cheek, referring to the cold snap in the UK. He plays with aplomb; the main piece is Beethoven's sonata in C minor, the *Pathetique*. The recital is flawless and serene, a level of virtuosity comparable to a show at London's Wigmore Hall or the Barbican. There you would have to pay good money, and have to put up with a late train journey home. To see him here I only have to take the lift down nine levels.

Schiller finishes at 3pm and I watch the sea for a while to kill time before a lecture by the Master Mariner Captain John Nixon in the Illuminations theatre. The sea, roused by a fresh south-easter at Force 6 (a "strong breeze" on the Beaufort Scale), is making quite large troughs and there are whitecaps. The waves made by the ship as it forges ahead create big collisions of water that rise up and subside in a white rush. The ship seems oblivious, just motoring on as stable as ever. It is probably using more fuel sailing into the wind and against the sea.

The talk is on what the Captain calls the 16th Century Astronauts, the intrepid mariners like Da Gama, Magellan and Drake who were brave and skilled enough to go where Europeans had not gone before. Nixon is surprisingly scathing about Christopher Columbus, remarking that he cannot understand why the Americans venerate him so much. He was a very bad navigator, whose calculation of the distance to China, his planned destination, was out by about 15,000 miles. He did not use the correct distance for the circumference of the earth and he never set foot in North America though he went to the Caribbean three times.

I expect a reaction from our American brethren but none comes. Of course, as it is a British speaker, Drake is the true hero of them all. The talk is a series of maps showing routes taken and brief remarks about each navigator; not as interesting as I expected. The American historian William Manchester, in his book *A World Lit Only by Fire*, a portrait of the late medieval period and the Renaissance, gives this flavour of those epic voyages, describing Magellan's crossing of the Pacific, part of the first circumnavigation of the globe:

"The little armada's 12,600 mile crossing of the Pacific, the greatest physical unit on Earth, is one of history's

imperishable tales of the sea, and like so many of the others it is a story of extraordinary human suffering, of agony so excruciating that only those who have been pushed to the extremes of human endurance can even comprehend it. Lacking maps, adequate navigational instruments, or the remotest idea of where they were, they sailed onward for over three months from November to March, moving northwestward under frayed rigging, rotting sails and a pitiless sun.

"Even for the age of discovery, Magellan's situation was unique. Previous explorers [including Columbus] *had known that if all else failed, they could always return to Europe. That option was closed to him. Ignorant of South America – having started from the mouth of a strait known only to him* [at Cape Horn] *– he had no base to fall back upon. Once he had left the eastern horizon behind, he had to sail on – and on, and on."*

After the harrowing tales of discovery I feel fortunate to be a 21st century seaborne traveller. I go on deck and take some last pictures of the wind-flecked sea, including a heavily laden freighter piled with containers on deck. I go to my cabin and get out my suitcase and start to pack. I take a break, have a shower and go to dinner. The talk is very general: Margaret went to dancing class and a tea dance. Roger talks about wills and lawyers, Leo about the latest wrongs by the captain of the *Costa Concordia* that was wrecked in Italy. Joe is more animated than usual. I do not say much, I already feel as if I have "left the building". They all shake my hand in farewell when we rise from the table. I notice no one suggests meeting again back in England.

The *Daily Programme* leaflet about disembarkation tomorrow does not mention a new time for self help passengers who get off with their luggage as I planned to do. We have lost our slot because the ship gets in later and guests going on excursions get priority to disembark. The Deck 12 group to which I belong is due in the Queen's Room at 10am. I go to the Purser's office to consult them and decide to go back to normal disembarkation. I will pack and put my bag out tonight, go through immigration, collect my bag in a tent on the dockside and then do customs.

I go back and finish packing and put my bag outside my door for collection. Later Dong knocks on the door and says no one will pick up my bag because they are only doing Decks 6, 7, 8 tonight. I explain my situation, that I am registered to disembark tomorrow, and he makes another phone call and knocks on my door to say it is straightened out and they will fetch my bag. Disembarkation has become a negative because of the confusion and changes of plan. This is also partly due to my obsession with getting organised in advance.

One major plus about our later arrival is that I am now reasonably sure that if I get up early enough I will have a good view of Table Mountain as we approach Cape Town. That was one of the things this trip was all about.

Tuesday 24 January

Disembarkation, Cape Town

I set my alarm for 5.30am but need not have bothered as I am wide awake from 4am. I get up, shave and get ready.

The suitcase I left outside my door has not been collected after all so I haul it back in. I am all dressed to leave the ship when I go up to see what's going on and where we are in relation to land. I climb up to the Observation deck but it is closed due to high winds, so is Deck 13. I rush to Deck 12 aft through the poolside doors but nothing can be seen from there and the forward raised level of Deck 13 is also closed. The only place left is the popular Deck 7. I go down in the elevator and a small knot of people are peering ahead from the forward rail of the port side with their cameras ready but nothing to photograph.

It is daylight and the sun is coming up behind a bank of clouds. The clouds are behind and covering Table Mountain dead ahead, a long dark clump that envelops the eastern horizon in an otherwise blue sky. There is no view as I imagined it, of the grandeur and flat-topped symmetry of Table Mountain and its two sentinel peaks floating improbably on the sea horizon at our approach. I must fall back on Harold Nicolson's first impression.

"At 10.0 we come up on deck again. There, straight in front of us, but still some miles away, lies a jumble of peaks and sugar loafs and in the centre a long blue precipice with its summit drawing a sharp straight line against the sky. 'That', I remark to V, 'is Table Mountain.' Each of us was taken by surprise. We had seen many photographs, films and paintings of this natural phenomenon, but had never yet realized how vast, how proud, how dramatic, it really was. This confirms me in my belief that no pictorial representation of the works of nature can communicate the actual impression, owing to the fact that no photograph or painting conveys the proportions of scenery

or the true relation between masses. One must always see places for oneself . . . Solitary, dominant and superb. It is coloured indigo and there is not a cloud upon its straight dark upper rim. 'But this,' I exclaim excitedly, 'is better far than Rio or the Bay of Naples. Why is it that nobody had ever told me about Table Bay before?'"

The QM2 is making a slow approach to the mass of sun, cloud and mountain that marks Cape Town. I think the harbour and city bowl are straight ahead but as time goes on Lion's Head emerges as a solitary pinnacle in the swirl of cloud and I see we are south of the Peninsula, approaching from the Robben Island direction off Sea Point.

I meet Dennis on deck and we commiserate about the lack of the view. He wants to know where Sea Point is as he is going there to see a friend. The residential towers of Sea Point are visible lining the shore. I explain to him the layout – we are looking at Table Mountain end on. As we slowly progress closer to land the clouds become less dense over the mountain and the familiar scene starts to open up. Devil's Peak is still covered but there are only wisps of cloud over the cable station at the top of Table Mountain.

I receive a text from Val . "Morning, we are watching the ship come in in front of the port control tower." They are in fact down at the docks near the navigation tower but I mistake her meaning, thinking she can see the ship in relation to the navigation tower from her house overlooking Table Bay. She texts again: "Where are you?" and I reply: "On the main deck front at the railing." She texts back "Wave", which I do, perplexed that she thinks she will be able to see me from her house up the slopes of Table Mountain.

The ship passes into the harbour and I might have seen Val and Stephen if I had known they were there on the jetty somewhere. The sun is out and the morning mists of the mountain are dissipating. By the time the ship has docked at 8am Table Mountain with her guardian peaks have completed their dance of the veils and are revealed in all their magnificent presence of grey rock, sheer bulk and vertical reach, truly the embodiment of the "Fairest Cape", as Sir Francis Drake described it. The ship is docked in a position that affords a wonderful close-up view.

On the dockside a large marquee has been set up as a customs house and tour buses are massing. There is lots of space and private vehicles are being parked in rows. The welcome is impressive, with bustle and purpose. A group of musicians approach with brass instruments glinting in the sun. With a banner saying "Welcome to Cape Town" they start playing in the spontaneous, joyful but imprecise manner that is the trademark of Africa. Everyone on deck cheers and applauds.

An announcement says the ship has been made fast and passengers going on excursions should start assembling in the Queen's Room to go ashore. I decide to have some breakfast as Val and Stephen, who have been up since 5am to greet the ship, said in a brief cellphone call that they are going somewhere to eat at the Victoria and Alfred waterfront. I am just sitting down to my last sausage and omelette when the announcer says the queues for disembarkation have cleared and now may be a good time for the rest of us to go ashore through immigration.

I go down to my cabin and take leave of it for the last time, saying goodbye to Dong on the way. By the time I have wheeled my big case down to Deck 3 the queue to get off stretches all the way from the front of the ship to the back. Jokes are being made about there being "no queue". Anyway it goes remarkably quickly and I am soon in the Queen's Room to have my passport stamped.

I trundle my bag down to Deck 1 and am signed out. My boon companion, my passenger card, is taken away from me. We are held up at the gangway for a short time for safety reasons while heavy equipment on the dockside crosses the path used by pedestrians. In the marquee an officer rummages through my hand luggage looking for fruit that cannot be brought ashore. Soon I am through and standing in the hot Cape sunshine waiting for Val and Stephen.

They soon arrive in their white SUV and we have warm greetings and much to say. Stephen takes pictures of Val and myself with part of the ship in the background. We drive through the docks and into the city. I am struck how prosperous and "scrubbed up" Cape Town looks. There are smart new cars, the streets are clean, the buildings newly painted and in good repair. Leaving the city centre we go up Orange Street into the suburbs that cluster at the foot of Table Mountain.

Val and Stephen's house is high on the slope. We carry my things up steep steps to their garden terrace and into the house. My room is at the back with a view of the mountain looming very close. The south-east wind is coming back and clouds are forming on the summit. We spend time sitting on the stoep, the front veranda, talking and catching up with the news. My nephew Simon's fiancée, Michela, drops in to see Val. She is surprised and delighted to see me as she did not know I was due today. I last saw her when we took her and Simon on a day trip to Salisbury Cathedral in Wiltshire in the winter of 2008. Michela makes herself useful by helping me connect my laptop to Val's internet router and I can do my first email to S using webmail. Once Michela has left Val makes sandwiches.

Later we go for a walk at the top of Molteno Road where the street ends at the foot of Table Mountain. The views are magnificent; on one side the mountain, on the other the city bowl down to the high-rise buildings and the harbour, with the *QM2* lying large, white and grey in her dock. I have seen the mountain from her decks and now on the same day have seen her from the mountain.

Around us lie large and small boulders littering the slopes among the scrub as far as I can see, like apples that have fallen from a giant tree. I am reminded of a description of Cape Town by the South African poet Anthony Delius:

Above all broods the burnt and buckled Table
At whose steep foot the crumbs of boulders lie . . .
And from the mountain's dolomite reflectors
Heat ricochets below to burn at will
The necks of businessmen and meat-inspectors
And bleach the beards of goats on Signal Hill.

The boulders and reflected heat have jumped off the page and are here with me. I bask happily in the sunny surroundings. Hundreds of parked cars sparkle along the Tafelberg Road where the lower station of the Cableway is situated. The suspended gondolas glide up to the structure on the summit, a dark speck.

The slopes below the lower cable station are covered in *fynbos*, the Cape flora that is unique to the tip of Africa; leathery protea leaves, feathery shrubs and spikey grasses. The paths are fairly level along the contours of the slopes, and dry and firm underfoot compared to England's muddy paths. In all my visits to Cape Town I didn't know there was this wonderful wilderness for walkers and bikers sandwiched between city and mountain.

Back at home I go to bath and Val makes *bobotie*, a favourite Cape dish of curried mince. We eat in the kitchen on a marble topped table that I remember from the farm in the Free State where I grew up. As small children we used to lie on our backs on it while our mother washed our hair in a basin. S phones from Farnham, landline to landline, and we have a good catch-up.

The south-easter is blowing in earnest again, whoofing and rushing round the house and down the chimney where we sit in the living room talking and reading.

Chapter 5

Cape

Wednesday 25 January – Saturday 28 January

Cape Town

*F*or four days I am Val and Stephen's guest. They have planned an itinerary to give me a grand tour. On the first day we set off for the seafront where a new football stadium was built for the World Cup football tournament in 2011. A new park to showcase Cape flora was created beside the stadium complex on Green Point Common. Val and Stephen are proud to show me an aspect of Cape Town I have not seen before.

The park features colourful but hardy drought resistant Cape flowers, blue agapanthus and aromatic perennials. It has a pond fed by a spring, a revived natural lake. More than 100 years ago the original freshwater lake was filled in to make land for soldiers and prisoners on Green Point Common during the South African War. Now it has been restored as a wetland and the park is a celebration of diversity.

Val shows me the "fan walk", a pedestrian pathway from the railway station in the city centre to the new stadium along which thousands of people streamed on match days during the World Cup. Val and Stephen started as bystanders until their children suggested they join in. As a result, something they were apprehensive about became one of the highlights of their life as they mingled with the fans from around the world, catching the World Cup fever. Val said it was such fun they encouraged their friends of the same age to join in, and they too were glad they did and were disappointed when it was all over. Embracing change reaped unexpected fulfilment.

Looking about me, Cape Town appears clean, bright and well organised. Who in the new South Africa is responsible for all this orderliness? Western Cape province is governed by a pragmatic middle of the road political party, the Democratic Alliance led by Helen Zille, who happens to have been on the Press Gallery in Parliament with me in the late 1970s. She was political correspondent of the Johannesburg morning paper, the *Rand Daily Mail*. The newspaper was staunchly anti-apartheid. It eventually closed down under harassment from the Government. In her day Zille was a star reporter, often scooping her male competitors.

Val and Stephen say Zille is very popular; she goes walkabout to see people on the street and is open for discussion. She is admired for her accessibility, issuing regular newsletters, doing emails and writing political commentary for newspapers. Compared to we who made an exit from South Africa, I admire her for staying on and making such a difference.

On another trip we visit Muizenberg on the Indian Ocean side of the Peninsula, in its time a fashionable seaside resort. Its waters are slightly warmer than on the Atlantic side. It has a gently shelving beach with white rollers suitable for surfing. We park in a municipal car park and an attendant approaches us about keeping an eye on our car. Wherever you park on the street someone in a yellow bib will approach; either they will keep an eye on your car in return for a voluntary tip, or they are paid by a security firm contracted by the city council to do the same duty.

This man is paid by the council because it is a park and ride area, but of course a tip would be welcome so he makes himself known to us. I ask him if this is the best job he can get. He says he does it because it is so difficult to find steady work. He is from the Congo Republic so is treated as an outsider. "I want to go Europe," he says, "there they give respect." I tell him Europe is too cold, crowded and confusing. I advise him to put his faith in South Africa which is No. 1 in Africa. He is unconvinced and says he is part of a group and they are going to Europe. I wish him well and shake his hand.

We cross the railway line and set off on a seawall path that runs above the rocks of the shore and beside the railway, towards Kalk Bay. The sea is a greenish colour and the rollers dash up white on the rocks. We come across a man in uniform at the door of a hut marked Shark Patrol. He has binoculars and an air horn. He tells us a shark spotter is located on the mountainside behind him. If a shark is seen, a warning is sent down and he takes action to warn anyone in the water.

They have flags with a shark logo in different colours for different conditions. Today the warning is a black flag for danger, meaning sharks can't be seen due to turbulence and the glare off the surface. After a chat with the shark man we reach a small secluded beach below the railway with a tidal pool which looks inviting. The water is warmer than the ocean because it is shallow and relatively still. Toddlers and their mothers play on the edge in the sand.

On the way home from Muizenberg we see some men who don't look too prosperous sawing timber in the heat under the sparse shade afforded by small trees. Stephen explains they are cutting an invasive wattle species from Australia, reducing it to firewood and selling it for their own income. In the old days I remember black people cutting down trees would be locked up, let alone being able to keep the proceeds. Everyone now at least has some economic opportunity, the sellers of trinkets and fruit at traffic lights, the sidewalk artists, the boys who collect errant golf balls and sell them on.

On the evening the QM2 is due to leave Cape Town, Stephen phones the port authority to find out what time she sails. We plan to drive to the top of Signal Hill to see her off. The vantage point will afford a view of her departure from Duncan Dock and her progress past Sea Point and round to the south east. Val cooks sausage and prepares a picnic. She arranges for Simon and Michela to meet us on Signal Hill. We pile all the gear into the car. I take my camera but forget my binoculars.

There are hundreds of cars on Signal Hill lined up along the railing of the road overlooking Green Point Common to see the ship sail. We find a parking place and walk back to find a place to watch from. The minutes tick by and through Val's binoculars we can see the ship is still firmly tied fast to the dock at 6pm which was when she was meant to sail. People are speculating on what is holding her up. Passengers late from excursions? Engine trouble? Someone who has been listening to the radio news says her departure has been delayed to 11pm, but offers no explanation.

By 6.30pm we discover the reason. Simon, an experienced yachtsman who knows his way around the port, manages to get through to the harbourmaster's after-hours number. He finds that it is the south-east wind that has caused the postponement. The wind speed is more than 25 knots, above the limit the authorities deem safe for ships to depart the dock. The Force 7 moderate gale (27 – 33 knots) blowing on the huge side surface of the *QM2* would make it risky to manoeuvre. Simon says the port authority might be stuck with the liability if they let her sail and an accident occurred.

I go round the corner of the road to take pictures on the Table Mountain side of Signal Hill and find that I have moved from a sheltered place into a gale force wind.

Here it is gusting so hard I can hardly keep my hands still to take a picture facing into the blast. My hat flies off my head and I have to sprint to catch it. We decide to go home for our picnic, it is blowing too hard. We are all disappointed as we look down on the ship that remains resolutely moored.

I can picture life on board. The first sitting in the Britannia restaurant would be in progress, the sun slanting in the windows with Alexis taking orders, the Russian wine steward dropping by to see if anyone wants wine, the conversation and swopping stories about Cape Town, the speculation about the consequences of the delayed departure. On deck it could be too windy for anyone to go out, least of all on the Observation platform. I wonder who Dong has got in my cabin to look after now.

The next morning when I wake up there is no sound of wind. I look out and Table Mountain is serene and calm in the sunlight with no telltale cloud that signals a gale. I wonder if the ship sailed in the night; I hope I have not missed it. When I look out of the front window, she is there in the same place. Back in bed, it strikes me that as it is a calm, still morning, fine and cloudless before sunrise, she will most likely sail at 6am, making her delayed departure an even 12 hours, a time lag that can be made up. She would not have attempted to depart at night.

I go back to the window and look again. I am fairly certain she has moved. I go into Val's bedroom and call her name softly but there is no response. I go back to the window and the ship has virtually disappeared from the frame, so she is definitely on her way. I go back to Val and gently rock her, saying her name. She wakes with a start and is surprised to see me. "The ship is sailing," I say urgently. "Come and see." She is suddenly as keen to see the sailing as I am and rouses Stephen.

We pull on clothes. We leave within ten minutes of me waking them. "I'll thank you later," says Stephen grumpily from the passenger seat as Val drives down Glen Crescent, past Lion's Head to Signal Hill. Pulling up at the roadside and jumping out, we see the *QM2* just departing the Duncan Dock entrance with her dark grey bows pointing out to sea. She looks big even from here, badged with white and red, her classic lines lending distinction. The morning is very beautiful and still, it is too early to be busy and noisy. The sea is deep blue, the city gleams in the rising sun, and the mountain ranges in the far background glow in graduated shades of lavender.

The only other person there is a man in tie and shirtsleeves who I guess is a professional photographer. He has a very big photo lens and uses a one legged stand as he takes pictures. I want to ask if he is a news photographer and what he's up to but he clearly is in a hurry and does not want to be detained. He heads off in his car after about 20 minutes of picture taking. By now the ship has been relieved of the two tugs that saw her out and the small pilotage boat leaves her side and heads back to harbour.

The *QM2* is once more under the spell of the sea. She moves slowly and deliberately on a surface so still the exhaust from her funnel rises vertically. I watch her as she scribes a wide arc round to our left, passing a marker buoy we can see through binoculars, past waiting freighters and into the channel that separates Robben Island from Mouille Point. We shift our position to an observation platform by the car park and follow her passage south-eastward.

While we are standing there a woman with a bulldog in a shiny black Lexus pulls up beside us crossways over three parking spaces. She leans out and calls, "Is that the ship?" She gets out leaving the dog in the car and starts asking questions about the ship which we happen to be well qualified to answer. She phones her husband at home in a seafront house in Camps Bay to tell him to get out the binoculars and take a look. It is clear he initially has no idea what she is talking about. When I say I sailed to Cape Town aboard her, she stares in amazement, as if I am Cortez landed in Mexico. She wants to know who we are and where we are from.

She has just been on her morning run and there are patches of perspiration on her shirt. We have an interesting and quite revealing chat for 15 minutes: how wonderful Cape Town is, how it is the only place to live, how her daughter in New York is sick and pining for home in minus 16C weather. She introduces herself, shakes hands all round and says goodbye. It seems to me that in a relatively small society of like-minded people with common interests, every stranger is a friend.

The *QM2* is now effortlessly overtaking a freighter piled with containers going in the same direction. I can see the white water under her bows, the same restless stream that used to fascinate me as I looked down from Deck 7 or Deck 13, or through the portholes outside the Illuminations theatre. She is clearly fully under way, probably 21 knots. I have now certainly seen her from every angle. My last sight of her is as a small shape on the horizon beside the slope of Lion's Head. I take my last ship-related photo, a white speck, and say farewell.

Stephen estimates she is already off Hout Bay on course to bypass Cape Point on her way to Cape Agulhas. I again imagine all the types on board, taking pictures of the Peninsula from the railings, queuing for coffee, fruit and breakfast in the King's Court, doing their morning exercises on the sundeck, and lolling on the loungers staring at their Kindles, here at the outer limit of Africa.

We go back to the house and I get ready to go out for the day on my own for the first time. Val drops me off at the Mount Nelson Hotel where the red open top tour buses go along Orange Street. They run every 15 minutes. It costs R140 (about £14) for the day, hop-on and hop-off. I get a set of red-wired earphones and sit on the upper deck in the sun. An attendant sets me up with the audio system, jokingly asking me whether I want Japanese as my language of choice. The earphones plug into a pod beside the seat where you can choose any world language and adjust the volume.

The commentary is uncannily accurate to where the bus is located notwithstanding delays at traffic lights and other variables. It is informative and entertaining, interspersed with catchy African music like *Nkosi*

Sikelel' iAfrika, the ANC and now national anthem, and numbers from the acappella group Ladysmith Black Mambazo. We go through District Six, an inner-city neighbourhood with a long heritage and an infamous history.

In the name of cleansing the "white" city, the apartheid government in the 1970s moved the population of about 60,000 mainly coloured people elsewhere to the Cape Flats outside Cape Town. It bulldozed the neighbourhood, destroying lives as well as heritage housing stock that would now be priceless. Today it is still a wasteland.

The outrage scared off any private developers so it has been an eyesore for more than 40 years. The only building of any note was Government-owned, a technical college for white students, now of course multi-racial. When I covered Parliament as a reporter I remember hearing Marais Steyn, Minister for what was called, in all seriousness, "Community Development", saying that District Six had to go because it was a slum. In fact the reason was the ideology of racial separation, the hallmark of Afrikaner nationalism.

With acts like the demolition of District Six, the apartheid politicians with their huge majority in Parliament, their sense of destiny, sowed the seeds of their own political destruction. In the late 1950s a Parliamentary reporter for the *Cape Times*, Anthony Delius, wrote a satirical poem, *The Last Division*, in which he describes from the Press Gallery the Afrikaner MPs "slowly chewing on a cud of power" with "balding crowns that planned the strangest laws".

God has through us ordained it so
Post Offices are split in two
And separate pillar boxes fix
That correspondence does not mix,
No one has ever managed better
To guard the spirit – and the letter.

The poem was banned from publication under censorship laws.

Back on the tour bus, at the Castle of Good Hope I learn that although the Cape changed hands between colonial powers several times, the castle itself never saw a shot fired in anger. It is squat and stone built, not particularly impressive, with each rampart named after a Dutch province ruled by the Prince of Orange. But it did have its share of violence. It has been a place of imprisonment, torture and execution of criminals. "Die Kasteel" was also where young men of my generation, including myself, reported for duty to do national service in the 1960s.

Along a rampart are arrayed the flags of the nations that occupied the Cape in turn; first the Dutch (starting in 1652), then the British, again the Dutch, then the British; then the Union, later Republic, of South Africa, and since 1994 the new non-racial South Africa. The Republic is once again a member of the British Commonwealth after leaving during the time of apartheid.

It is very hot on the top deck of the bus especially if it is not moving. I try going downstairs to the lower deck but then you can't see much so after a short while I go back to the top deck. I pass the attendant who is standing on the stairs halfway up holding a leaflet over her head as a shield against the sun. I tell her she has the best spot, half in, half out. She remonstrates with me for not staying in my seat while the bus is in motion.

Going up Long Street I learn that Lion's Head is called after the black-maned lions indigenous to the Cape. The species became extinct when the last one was shot in about 1840. We wind up Kloof Nek Road and on to Tafelberg Road where the lower Cable Station is located. I stay on the bus while most people get off. After a short while the bus turns round a traffic island and heads back down to Kloof Nek, a busy intersection on the saddle between Table Mountain and Lion's Head.

We go down to Camps Bay. On the way there is a dramatic view of the sea and the mountains overlooking the Atlantic. The mountain range is called the Twelve Apostles, for the number of rock buttresses in a row. There are in fact 17 "Apostles" so the name previously given by the Dutch, the Gable Mountains, seems more accurate. I had been to Camps Bay with Val and Stephen on my first day so I stay on the bus when it stops.

The commentary says Camps Bay is the upscale place for Cape Town nightlife, for celebrity spotting. Leonardo DiCaprio and Prince Harry have been seen here. The bus heads on in the hot bright sun with its motion making a welcome cooling breeze. We overlook the ocean washing up in white foam against the basements of luxury apartment blocks clinging to the cliffs. It looks chic and prosperous. This is Bantry Bay, where

Ambassador Walker, the speaker on the *QM2*, has his snowbird eyrie.

The Victoria and Alfred Waterfront forms a gentrified part of the Cape Town dockyard, a favourite with tourists. The bus commentary says people mistakenly call it the Victoria and Albert. But in fact the first dock was named for Alfred, Victoria's second son, who laid the foundation stone. Prince Alfred was in South Africa doing military duty in Britain's frontier wars against the Xhosa nation. The enlarged second dock was named after Victoria herself, hence Victoria and Alfred. Confusingly, later in the holiday, we will visit a town upcountry called Prince Albert.

In the central city I get off and walk along St George's Mall, which in the 1970s and before was a normal street for traffic but is now pedestrianised. It is filled with the market stalls of the new South Africans making a living by selling anything from souvenirs to electric batteries. The vendors sit contently about in the shade, eating crisps and scrolling their cellphones and talking, always chatting. It doesn't look a bad life. Some have their toddler children with them, amusing them as best they can. I go into the Cape Argus Building where I used to work when in Cape Town covering Parliament for *The Star*, the sister newspaper in Johannesburg. I want to get a back copy of the Tuesday edition that featured a front page picture of the *QM2* entering port.

The building is rather dilapidated and run down. It is now shared with the *Cape Times* which used to be a competitor, with its own building. The lady at the security desk signs me in, gives me a visitor sticker to put on my shirt front and a slip of paper that has to be signed by the person I am seeing and returned to her on my way out. I enter the lift with a young woman and ask if she is a reporter (I am so dying to see someone I know, that someone I don't know will do). She is indeed a reporter and she says she is on deadline (so don't keep me).

I tell her I worked as a reporter here 30 years ago but her eyes glaze over. I realise to win her interest I should have said something to do with her, like Who is the news editor now? or, Who is the editor? I go to the classifieds cashier and buy a back issue as well as today's paper to read what they say about the departure of the ship this morning.

The Tuesday paper has a good picture of the QM2 which makes it worth keeping. Today's paper briefly mentions the delayed departure of the ship. On an inside page it has coverage of the liner and features a picture of the barman who used to serve my Bass ales while I watched the football in the Golden Lion pub. It says he comes from Paarl, a wine-making town outside Cape Town. I read in the paper that the average age of passengers on the ship is 70 and there is an onboard morgue that can accommodate 40 bodies. They are unloaded at the next port of call for their families to collect. Well, I didn't see that in the voyage publicity.

Down in St George's Mall I try and identify the café where, in between deadlines, we Parliamentary reporters used to go to have a mid-morning breakfast, an occasional treat. I am not sure which it is but I think it is one now called Mint. It has outside tables under umbrellas in what would have been the street. With us was Tos Wentzel, political correspondent of the *Cape Argus*, who as the local person gave us the lead, Bruce Cameron, of the Durban *Daily News*, Leon Marshall of the *Pretoria News* and myself.

We were a fine band of collaborators. We pooled our copy for all the papers in the group and sought angles and stories of local interest for our respective readerships. There is now a piece of the Berlin Wall on display in the mall outside the café, another marker of dramatic change. The fragment, about 8ft high and covered in faded graffiti, was a gift to Nelson Mandela from the Germans.

On Loop Street I stop to ask a car guard what his duties are. He has a ticket issuing machine that he carries over his shoulder. He is employed by the council to sell parking tickets. Previously all the parking meters in Cape Town were regularly pillaged. Now wardens are placed everywhere to accept parking fees, issue tickets to be placed on the dashboard, while also serving as guards against vehicle theft. For the latter they expect a small tip.

The next day we go to Woodstock, to a must-see market called the Old Biscuit Mill which was also promoted in the commentary on the tour bus. We go into a hall packed with shoppers. The food stalls are for eat-in or take-home: Mother Shucker oysters, varieties of Cape grown olives from whole to tapenade, breads, fresh meat and fish, tarts and pies, cheeses and jars of green figs in syrup, honey and sushi.

The market is open only on Saturdays so the vendors are as keen to sell everything as their wares are fresh and tempting. The atmosphere is relaxed and fun: only an outsider like me, back like Rip Van Winkel after all these years, finds anything remarkable about the normal interracial friendships and goodwill.

It strikes me that those who elected to stay in the 1970s and 1980s instead of joining the mass exodus of white people, have now come through to quite a desirable settlement in their reconstituted city. I mention this to Stephen later in the day over drinks at home but he is not so sure, and non-committal about the reasons why.

During the course of the evening I exchange text messages with S who is at London Heathrow Airport ready for take-off to Cape Town. At departure time I enquire, "Sitting comfortably?" She texts back: "Yes – had some help to put case in overhead locker now all ready to fly – byee see u tomorrow x".

Chapter 6

Changeover

Sunday 29 January

Cape Town

*A*nother hot still morning; the temperature on the veranda is already 25deg before breakfast and is expected to go to 30deg during the day. I am excited at the prospect of seeing S; this is another changeover day in the holiday, including moving from Val's house to the Cape Paradise Lodge bed-and-breakfast nearby.

I pack my bag, leaving my jackets and dinner suit in the closet. I wear a new shirt and sandals with shorts. Going online on my laptop I find S's flight is 15 minutes early. I imagine it winging in over the Hex River mountains in the clear hot air.

We eat cereal and hurriedly leave earlier than we had planned. Val drives and the traffic is light at 8.15am on a Sunday morning. We go past the suburb of Pinelands where we rented a house one Parliamentary session. A bit further on there used to be a power station with huge cooling towers right by the freeway. The power station is still there though the cooling towers have been taken down. As with Battersea power station in London, no one is quite sure what to do with the site.

The townships that line the freeway have been substantially upgraded since I was last here. Being on the route to the airport in view of passing overseas visitors probably made it a priority for new state housing. Many of the shanties built with corrugated iron and recycled materials have made way for proper houses. Further on the shanties re-emerge but they are tidy. Tall poles with wires extending from them in all directions to the dwellings show that electricity has been laid on. Rows of portable toilets line the streets.

Cape Town International Airport, from which we left for Canada in June 1980, is very much a product and symbol of the new South Africa; paved, polished and bigger than normal capacity would demand. We park under a shady awning and walk the subways to the Arrivals hall. There are two British Airways jumbo jets on the tarmac outside the two-storey windows. One has just landed as the spinners of its engines are still turning. S has arrived.

As we wait, looking up at the sleek shape of the plane glinting in the dazzling sun I think of the great temperature changes the skin has undergone, from chilly Britain to sub-zero lower space to the burning tarmac of a Cape summer. There is a glass walkway from the plane so that disembarking passengers can see and be seen by those on the floor of the Arrivals hall.

We see S in her black jacket and jeans wheeling her case. I wave, and we all wave, but she does not look our way. She seems to be finishing a conversation with someone walking with her. After that it takes a while for her to appear – about 40 minutes, because her second case was one of the last off the plane. As she comes out we take pictures of her. I greet her warmly and take charge of the baggage trolley and we walk through the airport. We go home talking about her flight, the spectacular mountains set in the middle of a city, and the sudden sense of familiarity to her of the surroundings.

We have tea indoors in the living room where it is cooler than outside. S did not sleep much on the plane because it was so cold in the cabin and it did not warm up as the flight went on. She had to snitch a second blanket from the man sitting beside her. Memory of cold makes S appreciate the hot weather, which is a relief as I expected her to be complaining about the heat already. I told the guest house we would check in between 11am and noon. By the time tea is over it is 11.30. I go upstairs to finish packing, bring down my things and put them in the car with S's suitcases.

The guest house is located at the end of a cul-de-sac ten minutes' walk from Val and Stephen, but to get there by car it is a route of twists and turns, downhill and then back uphill. We were previously guests here in December 2006 and liked it for its proximity to Glen Crescent and its unassuming informality and cleanliness. It is run by a young German couple, Marco and Lena, and most of their guests are German tourists.

I press the buzzer outside the 7ft iron gates and Stephen drives in. Our host Marco is in shorts and singlet and lugs our bags upstairs to the Zebra Room, the same room as in 2006. The accommodation is done out in African animal themes. Our room has zebra lampshades and zebra masks on the wall in the bathroom. In the dining area lamp shades on the tables are made of ostrich egg shells carved in patterns. Outside, the pool sparkles blue.

Our room is clean and neat with white linen and bare pine floors. There is a balcony with a view of the city below. Marco gives us the spiel about breakfast times, using the honour system to pay for drinks out of the fridge in the common area, and how to contact him if something is needed.

He gives me a bunch of keys: a remote with a red button to open and close the entrance gates, a latch key for the front door, a key to our room and a key for the safe in the closet. We unpack. I leave quite a lot of stuff in my suitcase that I am unlikely to need. We go for a swim in the pool. At 1.30pm for lunch we walk down the road, about ten minutes, to an Italian restaurant at the top of Kloof Street. We share a very good salad and pizza washed down by cold beer.

It is marvellous for me to have the company of my wife again. I have lots to tell her about what the voyage was really like. She tells me news from home but nothing dramatic has happened. I find I am not missing Farnham yet. We go home to our room to get ready. Val and Stephen had told us they were going to church and would pick us up at 6pm to go to Glen Crescent for supper. By 5.45pm we are running late so arrange to walk. There are steps outside the iron gate leading up to a street behind the guest house. It is shady and cool on the streets among the suburban shrubbery. S admires the frangipani, the delicate white flowers tinged with yellow in the centre, and the flowers of the hibiscus. We pass a security guard in a wooden shelter, no doubt hired by residents to keep an eye on the neighbourhood.

Val and Stephen are getting a fire going for a barbecue. We sit outside as Stephen feeds sawn sticks from the garden. He pours chilled Castle beer from large 750ml bottles. We have the lamb chops from the Karoo, a part of the Cape we will be visiting next week. We talk about our lifestyles and how we manage, about family, the pleasures of grandchildren, and times past.

Stephen has only recently discovered undeveloped film from his wedding which took place more than 30 years ago. The prints show our daughter Lucy, age four, as a flower girl in the wedding party, and our elder son Guy in a smart v-neck sweater, age seven. That was a few months before we left for Canada in 1980. At the end of the evening we offer to walk to the guest house but Stephen insists on taking us in the car.

Monday 30 January

Cape Town

I wake up at 4am in the dark. The blind made of bamboo strips etches a pattern of light from the city below us on to the ceiling. It is warm despite the ceiling fan turning at medium speed.

Breakfast is in the dining area overlooking the pool, with a view of the city and the sea. The tables are placed close together each with a pair of wicker chairs facing each other. The Africa safari theme is continued with a neatly made ceiling of reeds. There is a porcupine quill in each napkin ring, and straw placemats. The space serves also as a lounge area with a TV; there are coffee- and tea-making facilities, and a fridge for alcoholic and fruit drinks.

Cooked and Continental breakfasts are on offer, ordered from and served by a woman called Patricia. Lena is there to say good morning and chat with guests, dispensing local knowledge and ideas for the day's sightseeing. We have bowls of fruit and cereal, make our own toast and serve ourselves coffee. It means popping up and down all the time to get this or that. The other guests are German but speak good English and we exchange news of our travels.

Val and Stephen pick us up at the front gate at 9.30am. We are going for a hike in the mountains behind Table Mountain, a nature reserve called Silvermine. The expected heat of the morning has been moderated by a northwest air flow which brings cloud and a cool breeze. In the Cape the south-easter brings heat and occasional gales while wind in the opposite direction off the Atlantic brings the rain in winter and relief from the heat in summer.

We drive out of the city round the base of Devil's Peak, past the University of Cape Town where Stephen attends summer school at this time of year. Most recently he went to a series on the South African War (1899-1902), a tragic period in the history of South Africa when the Afrikaners fought the British over the sovereignty of the Transvaal goldfields. After a series of setpiece battles, the Afrikaners took to the hills and waged successful guerilla warfare, while the British, whose immense Imperial firepower could not bring them to terms, resorted to burning their farms and putting their women and children in the century's first concentration camps, where 20,000 perished.

We reach the summit of the mountains dividing the southern suburbs from the rest of the Peninsula and turn off for Silvermine. Val uses her "Wild Card", a sort of pepaid subscription to nature reserves, to gain admission at the gate. We park the car, and Stephen leads us along well-made paths on a fascinating botany walk.

From a distance, when seen from the road, the mountainsides look barren. Once you are on the ground, they are anything but. The vegetation is rich and varied, studded with showy wild flowers. Close observation, a willingness to stop and look closely, is always rewarded, and we are fortunate to have Stephen as a guide. He and

Val live for being in the mountains, to walk among the flora and fauna.

The world has only six floral "kingdoms" and the Cape Floral Kingdom is one of them. This tiny part of the continent of Africa contains more than 9,000 plant species and 70 per cent of them are found nowhere else in the world. This is the *fynbos*, a word that literally means "fine plants", in the sense of "fine art". The Cape mountains, including Table Mountain, are made up of sandstones and quartzites originally laid down as sediments under primeval seas, giving rise to a unique collection of plants that are drought resistant and thrive on poor soils. They are also adapted to respond well to the frequent naturally occurring bush fires that sweep the slopes.

We see red stands of watsonias that especially thrive after fire. There are wild pelargoniums, blue agapanthus indigenous to the Cape, as well as orchids and heather. The landscape is made green and attractive by numerous large protea shrubs, the conebush that does not flower, the pincushion protea and the sugarbushes that produce the grand protea blooms adopted as the national symbol. These flower earlier in the year so we are too late to see them.

We walk to a viewpoint overlooking Hout Bay, a magnificent panorama far below us. It is a small fishing port and marina enclosed in a perfect crescent bay with a sandy beach. As we admire the view, Val serves *rooibos* (red bush) tea that can be taken without milk. We also have peaches. We head back on a circuit to the car, stopping to linger at the Silvermine dam where we see Egyptian geese and their young. The slopes overlooking the dam are peppered with picnic spots shaded by the keurboom trees where natural fireplaces have been built among the rocks.

We leave to go back down to the Blue Route shopping centre to visit the Checkers supermarket. Val is planning a family gathering and I volunteer to provide a Turducken, a combination of deboned turkey, duck and chicken. We pick up Roodeberg red wine to go with it. At Woolworths I buy a swimming towel. The beach towels on offer are garish pink and orange, probably what's left at the end of the season; so I buy a green bath towel. It costs as little as the ticket for the tour bus.

On the way back we decide to make a detour to visit the Rhodes Memorial. As we travel along Newlands Avenue to get there, I suggest we turn off and see the house our family rented in Hiddingh Estate until we left for Canada. We turn down Avenue La Caille and into familiar Finsbury Avenue. The house is screened by tall bushes and nothing can be seen from the security gate because of the high walls. S and I push through the bushes and look over the garden fence. The front terraces have been levelled and a pool built in the front garden, with a green lawn. The house is unchanged and I can see a piece of the view of Devil's Peak we enjoyed from our kitchen at the back. I snap off pictures of the front garden and we retreat.

Later S regrets not ringing the doorbell and meeting the occupants for a quick look around. It was very much her home because I was away in Pretoria covering politics for four months of the year, and she had to hold the fort and manage the children. She experienced frightening incidents: mysterious knocking on the front door when she was alone at night and her laundry being stolen from the washing line in the day. Some nights she slept in the same bedroom with the children. Other nights when she was particularly afraid, she took the children and stayed with a friend, Philippa Jordi, down the road. I regret S never told me of these things until we got to Vancouver.

We go back to Newlands Avenue and on up to Rhodes Memorial, driving through a peaceful wooded park above the university. Rhodes Mem, as it is called colloquially, looks north to the interior of the continent. It is a memorial to Cecil John Rhodes, perhaps best known today for the Rhodes Scholarships. He was a mining magnate and founder of De Beers, an ardent believer in British imperialism and Prime Minister of the Cape Colony at the time of the South African War. The granite edifice houses a bust of Rhodes and an inscription that Africa was in his soul. There are recumbent British lions like those in Trafalgar Square and the equestrian statue called *Energy* by the Victorian artist and sculptor G F Watts, which is replicated in another version in Kensington Gardens in London, and featured in the film *Rupture* I saw on the QM2.

Unsurprisingly, in the new South Africa the imperial shrine no longer seems much venerated. It is in need of a clean; the inscriptions on the granite are hard to read. Blocks of stone are sinking in the pavement. Today the memorial is being used as a set for a fashion shoot, with piles of equipment impeding the interior and skinny models being photographed in elaborate costumes. I hear them speak English in East European accents. We have tea on the terrace of a restaurant behind the memorial with a panoramic view of the cityscape, stretching across the Cape Flats to the mountains beyond.

We return to the guest house and later meet Val and Stephen at Bacinis, the pizzeria ten minutes walk down the hill. On the way home the waxing moon floats above the pinnacle of Lion's Head. When the moon is full, it is a popular activity to climb the peak in the late afternoon in time to watch the sun set on the western ocean horizon and watch the full moon come up afterwards. The excursion has become so popular that the peak becomes jam-packed, with the danger of people in the darkness being pushed over the precipices that surround the throng on every side. "We don't go up Lion's Head anymore, it is too crowded," says Stephen.

Tuesday 31 January

Cape Town

It is another bright warm day with sunshine streaming in the windows and a fine view from our balcony. We go for breakfast at 8.30am. Today it is Marco's turn to be on duty to greet guests. Once he has said hello and made brief small talk, he sets about tasks like putting things away and going out to sweep the bottom of the pool.

Afterwards, we head down the slope to the Mount Nelson Hotel via Hof Street to catch the red tour bus so that S can see the sights I saw earlier in the week. At Orange Street the bus is just pulling into the bus stop so we hurriedly dodge traffic to cross the road and have no wait at all.

Today the air is cooler than when I went, and the sea on the Atlantic side when we get there is much rougher with big breakers on the rocks at Bantry Bay. Unusually, and in contrast to the high daytime air temperatures, the Atlantic on Cape Town's shores is colder in summer than it is in winter. The prevailing south-easterly winds blow the relatively warm surface waters away from the beaches of the Atlantic coast and colder water wells up to the surface, making swimming in summer colder than it would be in Cornwall in the winter.

S enjoys the audio commentary and does not find it too hot. At the Cableway station we buy her bottled water. The commentary says the original inhabitants of the Cape, the KhoiKhoi herders, called Table Mountain "The Mountain in the Sea", with its dramatic setting so close to the ocean. It is somehow fitting that the turning point of the sea lanes at the tip of Africa is signposted by one of the most sublime natural landmarks in the world.

The bus terminates at the Victoria and Alfred Waterfront. In the curio hall S buys a string of freshwater pearls in greys and blues, neutral enough to go with most of her outfits. We go to the main shopping centre and buy postcards to send to family and relatives. I buy child friendly cards with pictures I can send to the grandchildren.

We buy books for Stephen and Val which we can give as thank you presents at the end of our holiday. A helpful assistant finds us a book on the South African War for Stephen and *The Help* for Val, the book, now a noted film, about black nannies bringing up white children in the US Deep South. I find a guide to the *fynbos* which I became interested in after yesterday's hike at Silvermine.

We have lunch at a waterfront restaurant and write the postcards while our food is being prepared. I have a toasted club panini and S the local Kingklip fish. Last night Stephen said he avoids eating Kingklip because it is being overfished. At the supermarket we buy a local pudding called *mavel* for dinner with the family tonight after S consulted Val on the phone. We walk to the taxi rank; the available car is a banger but we get in anyway.

The driver does not know Glen Crescent nor Molteno Road. I suggest he go up Hof Street, and give directions for the route. The drive includes the sights of downtown Cape Town which I point out to S. The car has no air-conditioning so we open the windows. The driver wipes his perspiring face with a cloth. The car barely makes it up the last steep part to Glen Crescent. The cost is R85 but all I have are R200 notes and R10s. The driver has no change. S comes to the rescue with a R50 and some change. Stephen is looking down at us from his front garden. We deliver the pudding for tonight. Val says she has leg of lamb in a slow cooker and is about to start roasting the Turducken.

We walk back to the guest house and relax before getting ready to go back to Glen Crescent for the family dinner.

When we return to the house my niece Marian is there helping her mother. Simon and Michela soon arrive. They are back from viewing the venue for their wedding at a nature reserve along the coast from Cape Town and have decided it will be ideal. Tonight to accommodate a crowd of 12 the dinner is to be held outside on the front lawn with tables and chairs set up on the level concrete of the garage roof that adjoins the lawn.

Stephen's brother Anthony and his wife Tina arrive, as does Stephen's sister Ida-Ann and her adult son Tivan. Later Marian's partner Luke, a doctor, returns from work at the emergency department of Constantiaberg Hospital. S brought a twin pack of Moet & Chandon from the duty free at Heathrow which we serve as a pre-dinner drink. This prompts excited comments as it is a great treat. "Real French Champagne!" they exclaim. Sparkling wine is referred to as "champagne" in South Africa.

We gather in groups for conversation and find we have a lot of catching up to do since we were last here in December 2006. Dinner is served, a lot of wine is drunk and the moon comes up over Lion's Head as the candles gutter in the wind. It is a convivial idyll of family friendships. In my mind the balmy evening contrasts starkly with the sub-zero weather back in Farnham, and the harder life.

Wednesday 1 February

Cape Town

We are awake by 7am and S goes down the corridor to make tea. Patricia is there and is keen to help. She has the milk jug ready to pour before the tea bag has had time to draw. Patricia says she has three daughters, two of them difficult teenagers. She rises at 5.30am in the townships to come to work on the bus. S tells her that's the same time she has to get up for work.

Breakfast is served from 8 to 10am. We place our order for a cooked breakfast with Patricia and chat with the other guests about Europe, the weather and what to do in Cape Town.

Today we go to Muizenberg to show S the seawall walk we did earlier to St James. In the car we discuss the family get-together of the evening before. One absentee was Anthony and Tina's son Carlos. He is part of the Handspring Puppet Company, the puppetry design and performance group started in Cape Town in 1981 and made famous by the stage hit *War Horse*. Carlos has given Val and Stephen a video of how the company worked with the directors of *War Horse* to design and construct the life-size horse puppets. They have not viewed the video, so we resolve to watch it together when we get back home. The play, put on by the National Theatre in London, was the inspiration for Steven Spielberg's film version, though the puppets were replaced by real horses for the silver screen.

We use the same Muizenberg car park and retrace our steps to the tidal pool on the beach at St James where we take off our shoes and paddle in the water. The Cape Town to Simon's Town railway line runs along the seafront and workmen are replacing copper cables stolen for their metal value, a problem also prevalent in

England. We take S to the Italianate seafront mini-mansion, the Casa Labia to see the artwork and have tea, before continuing in the car to Simon's Town. I did part of my National Service in the Navy here and it is much changed. For one thing, the naval uniforms of the new South Africa I see on the streets are quite different from the Royal Navy-inspired uniforms we wore.

Simon's Town was established by Simon van der Stel, a Dutch Governor who sought a more sheltered anchorage than Table Bay. The British built most of the current harbour infrastructure in the days when Simon's Town was the most important British naval base in the southern hemisphere. Britain ceded it to South Africa in 1957 as part of the post-war contraction of the Empire. My experiences in Simon's Town in 1963 included serving in a guard of honour for a visit by South Africa's Prime Minister, hearing the news of the shooting of John F Kennedy, and cleaning the seawater intake valves down in the bilges of the wooden-hulled minesweeper fleet.

Now the town is quite the tourist magnet. Street vendors are everywhere. We buy wireframe models of a lion and an elephant for our grandchildren in Alberta. For lunch we go to the False Bay Yacht Club which welcomes non-members. It has iron gates and a security guard who signs us in.

A short distance down the coast is Boulders Beach, a secluded cove with a jumble of enormous rocks surrounded by sand and water. We used to bring the children here to swim because the boulders form a breakwater allowing the nippers to paddle and play in calm water. Today there is a National Parks entrance charge and many more people. They come not only to use the beach but to see the small African penguins that congregate here. We all change and have a swim in the sea. The water is cold and refreshing. A mother Egyptian goose and a clutch of goslings swim in from the sea and clamber up the beach. Everyone is snapping their cameras.

We travel home on a circuit that takes us up Redhill road above Simon's Town to Scarborough. Val and Stephen are surprised to hear there is a seaside town of that name in Yorkshire. We pass a roadside stall filled with a startling array of large and small carvings of animals. Some are so big, like half lifesize elephants and 7ft giraffes; they would have to be specially shipped to get them home.

Crafts and carvings of more practical size are hawked at traffic lights. On offer by vendors walking up and down the lines of stopped vehicles are models of cars and aeroplanes made from scrap metal and drinks cans. They show amazing talent in their construction. Stopping to negotiate and buy through the car window would mean holding up the traffic behind so intersections do not seem a convenient place to shop.

Thursday 2 February

Cape Town

The south-easter is back. There is a gale blowing out there. Lying awake in the dark I listen to the sounds of the wind. The rushing sound comes and goes, a strong burst and then a lull. Just as in an orchestra, there are several sounds at once. The rushing sound is accompanied by an occasional whistle as the wind finds a flute. Sometimes the rushing turns to a low boom like a double bass.

Then a lull lasts for a minute or more and it seems the wind has subsided, but it suddenly resumes its headlong rush. Bizarrely in the chaos of wind, you can still hear the unruffled chirrup of birds delivering their normal dawn chorus. Instructions in the room warn guests not to leave their windows and doors unsecured when they go out, in case the wind plays havoc. But for the most part I notice Capetonians are unaware of the south-easter. It is as much part of their lives as constant rain was to us in Vancouver.

At 7.15am I hear a text message come in on my phone. It is Val saying that Helen Zille is on TV. The party leader and premier of Western Cape, once my competition in the Press Gallery, is addressing a business breakfast meeting at the Cape Town Convention Centre. I pull on shorts and go to the dining area where there is a TV and manage to quickly find the right channel.

She looks good – older of course, about 55, in her prime. Her hair is a bit mussed from the south-easter but she would not be the sort to worry about that. She speaks carefully and deliberately, sometimes glancing down at her notes but mostly off the cuff. There are no verbose party political boilerplate statements. She glances at her watch to keep time in a diligent, considerate way. She says the greatest challenge facing South Africa is grinding poverty and unemployment. Her party, the Democratic Alliance, has been looking at how other developing countries have encouraged growth – she mentions Malaysia, Turkey and Argentina. Her target is an eight per cent growth rate for South Africa. This will not happen unless the human resources represented by the unemployed can be harnessed.

She says she has good relations with the ANC national government, and with the President, Jacob Zuma. They can agree on a plan of action. However, though there is a collective will, when it comes time for action the capacity of the government is often too weak to deliver. Zuma instructs his civil service, but little or nothing is done because the bureaucracy does not know how to implement ideas and they get lost in the system. It is not leadership that is lacking, but know-how.

But I expect it will come right eventually. I was reminded at some point during my visit that when the National Party of the Afrikaners took over in 1948, they pushed forward Afrikaans people to displace the old guard British civil servants, in the same way that black people are being encouraged into the civil service by affirmative action today. I suspect in 1948 when the Afrikaners came to power the new era civil servants would also have had a lot to learn.

S phones our friend Peta at Cape Agulhas and they have a chat and confirm our arrangements for arrival tomorrow. We go to breakfast. The guest house is full. The German couple next to us had to wait two nights at the expensive waterfront Victoria and Alfred Hotel before they could get a vacancy here.

Today S and I are to visit Robben Island and see the high security prison in which Nelson Mandela was held for 18 of his 27 years of imprisonment. We leave at 9.50am believing we can make it by bus down to the harbour to catch the 11am ferry. But once at the bus stop on Orange Street I can see we are running out of time. I flag down a cab and he drops us off at the Waterfront. We have time to draw cash at the bank machine and buy our tickets before boarding. The terminus is called the Nelson Mandela Gateway. It is the starting point for visits to the former prison, now the Robben Island Museum, a World Heritage Site.

In a high wind that makes whitecaps in Table Bay, we sail on a catamaran ferry called *Sikhululekile*. Our fellow passengers, numbering in the 100s, are mainly foreign tourists and black South Africans. The seating is airline style and there are video screens showing historic prison scenes with a commentary. The catamaran bucks on the waves with the wind at its back. We dock in the shelter of a breakwater and are directed to a fleet of buses. We walk on the quayside where shackled prisoners, shoeless and underclothed, would have arrived to serve their sentences.

Even in the summer sun the wind is cold off the icy sea. The island is shaped like the back of a giant turtle that just died in the sea and fossilised. There is no high point or outcrop that would give shelter from the chilly winds that constantly sweep over it. Table Mountain and the mainland look a long way off, hidden in a white cloud.

We are on the island of outcasts, a bleak outpost used as a place of banishment for 300 years.

The first prisoner here was a 17th century KhoiKhoi who objected to the confiscation of his cattle by the Dutch, for which he was exiled to Robben Island. Somehow he managed to escape, the only man ever to do so. In the 19th century the British used the island to imprison the proud and blameless Xhosa chiefs they defeated in the frontier wars, including Maqoma, Siyolo and Xoxo. These were the forerunners of the 20th century Xhosas like Sobukwe and Mandela who rebelled against white rule and were also imprisoned here.

Each bus is staffed with a guide who gives a commentary as we tour the island. The guides are ex-political prisoners who live on the island in the houses once occupied by the warders. First stop is the leper graveyard, from the days when Robben Island was a leper colony in the 19th century. At each stop we get a lengthy and often amusing commentary. Our guide specialises in establishing our nationalities and making sardonic comments, like blaming the Australians for the gum trees, or pointing out that every nationality has some connection with Robben Island and therefore some responsibility. He says he had the privilege of showing Barack Obama round when Obama was a US Senator.

We stop outside a neatly tiled house inside its own tall fence. This is where Robert Sobukwe, leader of the Pan Africanist Congress, a breakaway group from the African National Congress, was kept in solitary confinement. He led a protest against the pass laws, which restricted the movement of black people, and was imprisoned for three years. When time came for his release, the apartheid government inserted a "Sobukwe clause" in the General Law Amendment Act to allow for his continued detention without trial. So he was sent to jail in case he committed a crime in the future. The progressive MP Helen Suzman gained special permission to visit Sobukwe here. When our guide asks who the white liberal MP was, S is the only one who comes up with the answer. Our guide is impressed.

The time on the bus is becoming lengthy and cramped. With the constant harangue of the guide I am starting to feel I am in a mild detention myself. The tour takes us past nine churches, the Governor's house and a gun turret from the Second World War. Finally we are released off the bus to enjoy views of Table Mountain across the wind streaked sea, with rollers bursting white on the black rocks that rim the island.

We drive to the limestone quarry where Mandela and other prisoners toiled in the heat and glare. Our guide says this is where powers of leadership were forged in conditions of hardship and deprivation. Yet the tone of this leadership was of reconciliation, the same power of compromise shown by Mahatma Ghandi and Martin Luther King. The Robben Island prisoners educated themselves and each other through correspondence schools. President Jacob Zuma, who was imprisoned here for ten years, had only four years' schooling when he came to Robben Island and left with a degree. In his day if a youngster could count the number of his father's cattle he was deemed to be educated enough.

At the main prison block we walk into what was once a communal cell where a different guide, also an ex-prisoner, describes what conditions were like. He holds up a board showing the weekly rations and tells us that until 1977 political prisoners were not allowed bread, only maize porridge. He remarks with some feeling: "We live in a Christian country in which we pray that each day we may be given our daily bread. Yet we black prisoners were given no bread." This applied also to Mandela and was changed only after pressure from the International Red Cross.

Black prisoners were not issued with underpants or socks and wore shorts, while Asian and Coloured (mixed race) prisoners had both underwear and socks, as well as long trousers. Prisoners in their cells during the day were not permitted to lie down, they had to be standing or pacing, in a cell about 5ft by 6ft. It reminds me of the Russian prisoners in the Gulag who had to sleep with their arms outside their blankets in their freezing unheated cells. There were no beds for prisoners on Robben Island: they slept on a blanket on the concrete floor. We see Mandela's cell with the blanket neatly laid out on the shiny concrete floor, a stool and a latrine bucket.

It is all rather shocking that this went on while I was living the easy life of a white man on the mainland. We were all deliberately kept in the dark: there were legal sanctions on any reporting in the media of prison conditions. On the catamaran back to Cape Town they show video footage of a press visit to Robben Island in the 1970s, a junket aimed at generating some positive coverage for the authorities. I recognise journalists I worked with in the Parliamentary Press Gallery, all looking rather earnest and gullible. I can say this with the benefit of hindsight.

There is also footage of the arrival in Cape Town of the first political prisoners released from Robben Island in 1991. Our ex-prisoner guide told us the ship used to transport them was a freighter; he said the prison authorities did not respect the people enough to transport them in a passenger ferry. Our ferry the *Sikhululekile* is leaping up and down over the waves in the teeth of the south-easter. One minute you can see just sky, the next just sea. Back on dry land at the Mandela Gateway in the gift shop, we buy a biography of Robert Sobukwe written by Benjamin Pogrund, a brave *Rand Daily Mail* journalist who exposed prison conditions and nearly went to jail himself.

After our brush with the moral dilemmas of South Africa, it is time to get back into a frivolous holiday mood. At the Victoria and Alfred shopping mall I decide to have a haircut at a smart men's hairdressing salon. This is no red pole barber shop and as a man of a certain age I am treated as if this is not the sort of place I would be expected to enter. At the next chair a young man in a singlet is having an elaborate bit of hairdressing involving clipping, colouring and massaging a mass of thick blonde hair. Earlier I had seen a customer at the back with cropped head having a skull massage. I get a neat trim from a young man with a diamond stud in his ear. He shakes my hand in greeting when we begin but says nothing further. I decide not to intrude on his trendy world.

I am pleased with the haircut. Suddenly the young man, without so much as a by-your-leave, sticks a warm plug in my nostril, like a cotton bud. He does the same to the other nostril so I have to breathe through my mouth. Then similar plugs are thrust in my ears. After a short interval he takes firm hold of the bud stem in my nostril, twists and jerks out all my nose hairs. He shows me the hair stuck to the waxed bud. It is more startling than painful. I won't have to clip my nose or ear hairs for a while; it has made me like a young man again.

We take a cab back to the guest house. Travelling up the last hill to the gates a workman from a building site steps into the road in front of the car and the taxi driver gets a fright followed by a fit of rage. Later we go to Val and Stephen for dinner, eating moussaka indoors. S admires Val's photo albums of her sweet children when they were young. Then we go home in the wind in Stephen's car. Tomorrow we set off on our road trip.

Chapter 7

Agulhas

Friday 3 February

Cape Agulhas

*A*s usual I am awake early in the dark. The wind has gone quiet, with only birdsong audible. Once the sun is up, outside on the balcony we look over the wind flattened canopies of the pine trees to a blue sky and Table Mountain clear of cloud.

I have previously arranged with Marco and Lena to leave our big suitcases with them until we return in a week's time from our road trip. I sort clothes I am taking from those we are putting in storage. S is also deciding what to take but it is much more elaborate for her as big decisions have to be made on what to wear. In the heat of the room with the sun streaming in, I make an assumption we won't need warm clothes. To every question from S I say, no you won't need that, too hot. But as we shall see, Africa will fool me.

I put our suitcases away in the neat garage where supplies are kept for the guest house. S later wants to take an envelope of photos of our grandchildren so I have to go back to the suitcases, open up and do a search.

S packs a medium size bag and I get all I need into my small bag. After all my chivvying we are early. While we are waiting at the gate Lena, who has come down the drive to see us off, tells the story of how they came to buy the bed and breakfast. They originally came to Cape Town as visitors then moved here to open a guest house. They were under pressure because they had to find a property, then keep to a schedule to make alterations and be ready to open for the summer season. After seeing more than 50 properties they decided on one even though it was not ideal. A chance conversation with a neighbour of the property they were buying led them to the current house which they think is ideal. Val and Stephen pick us up at 9.30am and we say our farewells.

We set off on the N2 national road, past the airport, across the Cape Flats to Somerset West, where my mother lived in retirement, and past Strand with its lengthy beach on False Bay. We turn off to take the coast road past Gordon's Bay where I did my naval midshipman's training in 1963. Looking down from the high level road it looks much the same. The naval base is jammed between mountain and harbour so there is no room for expansion and the buildings look the same as they were. That's where I learned some useful life skills – discipline, punctuality and how to iron a shirt.

Hugging the foot of the mountains we wend our way along an almost empty road above the bays and bights of the sea. We traverse a divide in the mountains to cross a peninsula and on the other side the weather changes from hot sun to cloudy and cool. We stop for tea from a thermos at Kleinmond where it is cool and breezy, sitting on a bench among *fynbos* overlooking the sea. S needs her fleece top and only brought her lightest one. She will wear it now every day. I am already in trouble with my weather forecast.

At the Visitor Centre they have a fine display of *fynbos* species. I discover that a grass I have been trying to identify is called Harestail (Haastert) *Lagurus Ovatus*. We press on towards Hermanus along rolling roads beside bare mountains damaged by fires. Black limbed skeletons of protea bushes contrast with white sand on the ground. The fire has scorched to the top leaves of gum trees.

Hermanus is a thriving place, straggling several kilometres along the coast. We stop off at Gearing Point to look at the view and see if any whales are spouting in the bay. We pass prosperous people having lunch on patios outside the restaurants even though the weather is grey. The British Union flag is flying in the grounds of a seafront hotel. I am reminded of the Lincolnshire golfers on the ship who were coming here for a lengthy game.

On the main road out of town we pass a waterfront house I stayed in with Val and Stephen in 1999. They used to rent it from a friend called John but John had a falling out with his family and no longer uses the house, so of course Val and Stephen are not invited to use it either. Stephen is driving and he lets faster cars pass by pulling over on to the hard shoulder. Once the car has passed it acknowledges by double flashing its rear amber lights. It is a common practice you see all the time on the trunk roads, making way for faster traffic.

We leave the mountains that rim the coast and enter a broad coastal plain. This is the Overberg. Harvested wheatfields roll white against the dark mountains in the distance. There is rain on the windscreen and dark clouds ahead. The heat and bright light of Cape Town are now a memory. We stop in a village called Napier for lunch at a farm stall. It is rather unusual with a dark interior, rusted farm implements for decoration and local produce like pickled green beans, exotic jams and unpasteurised honey. Fresh bread is advertised outside so we order sandwiches.

My chicken mayonnaise sandwich is quartered and skewered on a porcupine quill. S has toasted cheese and tomato. Crickets chirp inside the room, striking a dissonant note over the piped music of Frank Sinatra and Dean Martin. We reach Bredasdorp, one of those Afrikaner heartland farming towns, where time has stood still. We turn right to Struisbaai. It is a long straight road, very dull under a grey sky, lined with old trees full of dry pods.

It is raining in Struisbaai, cool and damp. We did not come prepared for this. On our way to Pebble Beach, the bed and breakfast run by Chris and Peta where we are to stay the night, we pass the southernmost tip of Africa, Cape Agulhas lighthouse, and take an unpaved road to Suiderstrand.

The village beyond Agulhas where Chris and Peta have their bed and breakfast is in a nature reserve beside the sea, green with *fynbos* and white with seashells. Pebble Beach is well signposted and I recognise the house from spying on them with Google Earth. I get out first and call out. The front door is open and Chris is sweeping the red tiled floor of beach sand left by previous visitors. Peta comes from upstairs. We greet and hug. We haven't seen them since they visited us in Maida Vale in London 12 years ago. Chris was a reporter with me in *The Star* newsroom in the 1970s. They became family friends, with Chris taking a hand in getting Guy to walk when he was a baby and becoming godfather to Lucy.

We have an evening of reminiscences. Chris was just talking of Ron Anderson, our news editor at *The Star* who is now in his 80s, when Ron himself phones from Johannesburg about something he sent Chris in the mail. I speak to Ron and give him a quick outline of my life after journalism. Chris tells me several former newsroom colleagues have written books. He shows me copies in his library that have been dedicated to him and signed by the authors.

Chris makes a barbecue with huge "Texan pork steaks", *boerewors* sausage and bacon. The cooking finishes in the dark amid much talking, laughter and wine. Afterwards I go to bed with a headache that increases as time goes on. In South Africa it is called a "babalas", from the Zulu word for the effects of overindulgence, *ibhabhalazi*.

Saturday 4 February

Nature's Valley

We are up at 7am and take a shower in brackish, hard water. The floor of the shower is attractively decorated with wide spaced pebbles, a motif repeated on the outdoor paving, reflecting the name of the guest house. We gather round a big table set for breakfast, and feast on giant slices of cantaloupe (*spanspek* in South Africa) and mangoes, exactly ripe for eating. Chris offers to make scrambled eggs; he does the cooking for bed and breakfast guests. Val and Chris have eggs, and the rest of us cereal and fresh bread made by Peta overnight in the breadmaker.

Breakfast conversation is about bird watching, a hobby in which Chris is clearly an expert and Stephen as well. The neighbouring nature reserve is a birding treasure trove. We say our goodbyes, regretting that the visit has been so short, but Val and Stephen are clearly interested in coming back as paying guests. Besides the bed and breakfast rooms on offer in the main house, Chris and Peta run a separate self catering cottage a short distance away close to the seafront.

The houses in these parts appear built to withstand stormy weather and gale force winds. They are blocky and strongly built of bricks and mortar, crouching in the bush. The chimneys have angular cowls that spin to face the wind direction so the wind does not go down the chimney. They look like large hooded birds brooding on the chimney tops.

It is still showery and cool and there are clouds on the distant mountains and overhead. After the long straight road back to Bredasdorp we turn for Swellendam to rejoin the N2. The country is vast and rolling under a big sky, made up mostly of harvested wheat fields interspersed with thorn trees, gum trees and shrubs. There are ostrich farms and sheep grazing the stubble; rather gaunt sheep compared to the tubby ones on English grass. At a place just beyond Swellendam called Buffelsjagrivier (Buffalo Hunt River) we stop for petrol at a BP station.

An attendant fills the car: no self serve here. He sets the pump going with the nozzle in the filler neck and leaves it while he attends to other customers and cleans our windscreen. The pump stops with a clunk when the tank is full. The attendant has one of those wireless card machines into which he slides my credit card. It is accepted here in this remote spot with my name neatly printed on the receipt – the wonders of the global marketplace. The charge for the fill-up is R471.46, which when I get my statement back in Farnham comes out at £40.90. A fill up in England would have been £60. I suspect petrol is cheaper because government duties are less.

The next big town is Mossel Bay which has been transformed since I was last here by offshore natural gas finds, making it the Aberdeen of South Africa. The processing plant can be seen from the road. This is one of the world's largest gas to liquids refineries, using gas piped from the offshore fields.

We see hitch-hikers outside the towns. They wave banknotes, indicating they are prepared to help with the petrol if they are picked up. This increases their chances of getting a ride. At a Total petrol station we stop for a picnic lunch outside the burger bar and coffee shop. Val produces buns, cheese and hard boiled eggs for sandwiches followed by peaches for dessert. From Mossel Bay to the town of George it is dual carriageway and quite quick. George has an airport and like Mossel Bay has also become much larger since we were here last, admittedly more than 30 years ago.

There is a notorious hill outside George that winds steeply down to Wilderness, crossing the gorge of the Kaaimans River. This is the divide between the dry brown Overberg and the vivid green climatic region along the coastal strip confined between mountain and sea. This is the Garden Route part of our trip, where the vegetation is lush, mostly natural forest. There is the rank smell of sea and bush and the landscape is hilly and studded with sheets of water which are either fresh water lakes or lagoons of mixed fresh and sea water. As a holiday playground destination it is an area of spectacular beauty that reminds me of the Lake District.

We travel through Sedgefield and on to Knysna. I am again surprised by how much it has grown. Roads have been realigned so they have no relation to what

I remember. I used to visit here with student friends when I was at Rhodes University, not far up the coast at Grahamstown. One night we drove around with a girl's head poked out the window trying to sober her up before taking her home to mother. Of course it did not work. Then later S and I were here on a tour when S was pregnant with our first born, Guy. It was our last holiday before familyhood. This year Guy turns 40.

Travelling on, pine plantations of young trees cover the foothills beside the road, growing the wood for furniture and flooring for generations of South Africans not yet born. We stop at Plettenberg Bay, at one of those outdoor shopping malls beloved of countries with lots of space. Val and S go to the Pick 'n Pay supermarket for groceries and I buy beer and wine for our stay in Nature's Valley. While I am waiting I fall into conversation with a mixed race Afrikaner who says he is down from Johannesburg for a funeral. I am surprised how my rusty Afrikaans splutters back to life and I have a passable conversation.

Not long after Plettenberg Bay we turn off the highway for Nature's Valley. I don't remember the turnoff because the layout of roads has been improved. We arrive in the Nature's Valley township screened by indigenous forest, all super natural. We go to see Val and Stephen's friends Erica and Sid, who own both the home they are staying in and the house we will be using. The couple live in Cape Town and spend downtime in Nature's Valley. Erica is a close friend of Val's. Sid is a former gold miner from Westonaria near Johannesburg who later became a technical college instructor. They are very friendly and welcoming. They have heard so much about us, we hope we can live up to it.

After tea on the deck we get the keys to our house and move in. The place is dark in the trees and the evening is cool and cloudy. But the house is cosy and has a magnificent second storey deck under a canopy of yellowwood trees. Sid built the house himself and the attention to detail shows. Trees that had to be cut down to make way for the house are used as supporting posts inside the house. Staves made from the brush of pine trees and stained with varnish are used for railings to enclose the deck and the stair banisters. A tree spirals up through the floor of the deck.

The house is normally let to visitors. With typical South African directness, there is a warning at the entrance: *BEWARE baboons! They will <u>ruin</u> your holiday and <u>trash</u> this cottage! Keep windows and doors closed unless you are in <u>that</u> room!*

Simon telephones from Cape Town with greetings and says the weather in Cape Town is hot again so we along the coast should get the good weather tomorrow.

Sunday 5 February

Nature's Valley

I was told bush pigs forage by night and monkeys by day. As I sit in the warm sun having my breakfast under the canopy of the primeval forest I am wary a baboon might swoop down and steal my *snoek* on toast. Snoek is a local fish with devilish bones that have to be picked out. It is very tasty when smoked, though it does not have the richness of the English mackerel. But no wild thing shows any interest in my breakfast and I am joined by the others.

We pull on our swimming gear and set off for the beach, walking through the township of holiday homes in a variety of styles, many quite rudimentary but located among beautiful flowering trees and green lawns. The beach is a vast expanse of white sand with almost no people on it. Breakers roll in, making criss-cross patterns of white foam, betraying the offshore undercurrents. Erica and Sid are there already and we settle down with them on a log washed up by the waves.

I immediately want to swim. The water is much colder than I expected, and full of bits of seaweed held in suspension. The storms and rain have stirred up the water. It is as cold as Polzeath in Cornwall, says S. We spend a short time in the water with the waves breaking over us and come out on to the hot beach to warm up.

S and I walk along the sand towards the area of houses where we stayed when we spent holidays here with Guy as a baby in the early 1970s. Walking on the yielding sand, even on the margins where the sea has compacted the wet surface, is hard work. From end to end the beach must be about four miles long and we walk about 2.5 miles of it. We find the row of houses in the prime position we remember, facing the lagoon formed by the entrance of the river into the sea. The incoming tide throws sand into the mouth and stops it up, then the river has to force a passage, burrowing through the beach to the sea, leaving behind a still lagoon of warm water, ideal for swimming and for children to splash on the edge.

The houses in the best position were the first built at Nature's Valley while it was a farm and before it was formally made a township. They are called the Syndicate houses and belong to a group of families who negotiated the leases in 1942. The cottage we stayed in looks just the same, including the shrubbery half obscuring it.

We rented it from the Jordis for a nominal sum. John Jordi was the editor of *The Star* in the early 1970s. He died of a heart attack at his desk in the office one morning. His widow Philippa was S's neighbour in Newlands (where S took refuge at night with the children). John took a shine to us and even lent us a canoe that we lashed to the roof of our Peugeot 504 and carried down the precipitous mountain passes to get to Nature's Valley.

We retrace our steps across the burning sands like explorers in the desert, back to our log. Erica and Sid have gone home. We have another swim to cool off. We return to our house along the grid-pattern streets and shower outside in the garden. It is a hot water shower behind a screen of palings. It is refreshing to rinse off the sea water under the forest canopy. S makes her famous tuna salad and we have it on the deck with glasses of beer. There is a bird called a loerie that I am told has remarkably beautiful markings. We often hear it but I never catch sight of it.

S decides she needs some downtime so elects to stay in to read and nap while Val and Stephen and I go for a walk. Stephen takes us to a forest called the Tsitsikamma and we take the Kalander trail, named after the local word for a species of tree, Outeniqua Yellowwood. The footpath is firm underfoot, covered in dry leaves. Over us looms the massed canopy of a semi-tropical forest. It is not particularly hot or humid in spite of the recent rain. Stephen takes us to magnificent stands of giant indigenous yellowwood, ironwood and Cape chestnut trees, some of them adorned with long strands of twining lianas. We visit the Groot (Great) River just above the lagoon to see a new bridge built to replace one that was swept away by floods that affected this whole coast in 2005. The water is clean and sparkling though attractively brandy brown from decomposition of vegetation.

Back at the cottage I find an interesting booklet *The Story of Nature's Valley* by Nora and Chris Sinclair.

"Tucked away in the fringe of a massive, indigenous forest and protected by deep, river gorges, Nature's Valley shimmers like a gem displayed in a perfect setting . . . Nature's Valley is the only township in South Africa that is surrounded by a national park and it can never be expanded into a sprawling conglomeration of housing. Most of the holiday cottages are simple and blend into the natural bush. Nature's Valley has become an exclusive holiday resort without the hotels, shopping malls, cinemas and nightclubs of neighbouring Plettenberg Bay."

The gorges and forests around Nature's Valley, the Bobbejaans (Baboon's) River, Groot River and Bloukrans

(Blue Cliff), presented a formidable barrier between the Western and Eastern Cape regions. In 1868 engineer Thomas Bains made a survey to see how and where a road could be built. There appeared on the scene a young man who lived in the forests, Hermanus Barnardo. He advised Bain to build the passes on the old elephant trails. Barnardo was the first permanent Nature's Valley resident, building a house facing the lagoon at a point furthest from the beach. He hunted in the bush, married three times and fathered 19 children.

Regular campers who spent holidays in Nature's Valley often begged Barnardo to sell them a portion of his farm. For years he refused. Finally he agreed to sell the small portion of the farm on which they regularly camped. This was the creation of the 1942 Syndicate in which 1.6963 morgen (about 2.5 acres) were transferred from Barnardo to the original ten Syndicate members: Le Roux, Van Hasselt, Dreyer, Hudson, Nash, du Plessis, McIntyre, van der Riet, Deneyssen and von Bonde, for a total purchase price of £755 4s 5d.

I discover the Jordi cottage was originally the only other dwelling besides Barnardo's farmhouse. It was built by Bill von Bonde, a professor of geology at Free State University in Bloemfontein. He called it *Seldom Inn*, the name it bears today. Back in London in a conversation I had at work with the chairman of Rio Tinto, South African born Jan du Plessis, he mentioned to my surprise that he goes to Nature's Valley every Christmas and New Year, an apparently sacrosanct engagement. I can now see why. A du Plessis family was one of the original Syndicate members, and these cottages are so valuable that they would never be sold outside the family. Erica told me the Syndicate members ritually gather at Christmas each year.

Erica and Sid arrive for supper, another barbecue. Erica brings marinated chicken kebabs and joints of meat and Sid fires up the *braai* (barbecue) with lumps of charcoal. Sid becomes our host in his own house. He says this is their dream home, lovingly created with his own hands. He tends the barbecue with great care, cracking jokes in English and Afrikaans. He is quite at home in both languages. He talks about the birds of the area and feeds a robin that flies down to perch near him. It has a fledgling which the mother bird feeds with scraps from Sid. Stephen is disconsolate as he can't find a much-prized jacket that he brought on the trip. Rather unkindly, Sid jokes that he saw a baboon wearing it.

We sit round the counter in the kitchen for dinner. Erica sets out place mats cleverly made out of recycled crisp packets. The Africans wind the silver paper tightly round kebab sticks then join the parallel lengths with thread to hold them all together. It is neat and ingenious with the names and brand images on the packets still partly recognisable.

We go through several bottles of wine. We talk about children and grandchildren, our contrasting lives in Cape Town and London, and past difficulties. Sid hurts himself bumping on the post that supports a beam above the counter. "Well, you put it there," says his wife.

Monday 6 February

Nature's Valley

I fry sausages for breakfast. While they are sizzling I go to the Nature's Valley shop about 15 minutes' walk away to buy eggs. But the shop opens only at 8.30am and this is 8.10am, so I go back and we do without. The shop has an adjoining pub and restaurant with tables set out on a patio under umbrellas. Outside an interesting signboard describes the habits of the whales that can be spotted from the beach. Back at the cottage we eat our sausage and bread breakfast on the deck. It is sunny and very pleasant.

While Stephen is mourning the loss of his jacket, S discovers she can't find her precious sunglasses. Nevertheless, we set off on a walk led by Stephen to Salt River mouth which is round a headland on the opposite end of the beach to the lagoon. We scramble across razor sharp rocks with the surf beating below and enter the cool shade of the forest on the way to the river mouth, clambering down a steep slope to get to the beach.

The brandy coloured stream meanders into a cove fringed with white sand. From above, the cove looks idyllic but there are sharp stones scattered on the sandy bottom which make it uncomfortable to swim. I go to investigate a place to swim in the river where it flows from a forested valley. Crossing the beach, I see eight dead sharks lying at the high water mark with flies buzzing around them. One has a gash over its head, the others look unmarked. We speculate that these were caught in the nets with other fish, killed and abandoned.

I find a pool of water in the river, deep enough for a wallow and a good cool off. Later we leave the beach and walk through the forest on a different route to the way we came, over the headland back to Nature's Valley. There are impressive views of the township and the beach fringed in white surf and blue sea. The sun is in the right place for panoramic bird's eye photographs.

The weather is clear, still and hot. Back on the beach we go for a swim to cool off but the water is very cold and all I can manage is a dip under and out. Despite the heat the only other person in the water is a surfer wearing a wet suit. Stephen gets used to the cold water and stays in a long time. Feeling the glare and heat of the beach, S and I go to the shade outside the shop and restaurant where the car is parked.

A young couple at the next car have just come off the Otter Trail which ends at Nature's Valley. It is a four day trek on foot through rugged and often wet coastal terrain that you have to book to go on far in advance. The couple say they had rain and trouble crossing the river mouths and are glad to have finished. They are looking forward to food other than noodles, as well as clean clothes and a dry bed. Val and Stephen did the Otter Trail last year, so when they join us they discuss the details with them.

We go home for lunch, and later Val and Stephen go to the lagoon to walk and swim, while S and I stay at home.

S finds a book on Wallis Simpson that absorbs her. I find S's missing sunglasses on the window ledge behind the blind. Later Stephen phones Peta in Agulhas and discovers he left his jacket there.

Val makes supper, the curried mince dish *bobotie*, with rice and baked butternut squash. We drink beers and wine. We look through Val's bird book to identify birds I saw in a garden during our walk, then we go to bed. We can't immediately sleep. Through the night there is a noise like running water in the plumbing. I worry the hot water tank is still filling after the dishwasher has finished and it might explode over our heads and scald us.

In the morning I find the next door bathroom extractor fan was left on. One switch, a hanging cord, controls fans in both bathrooms.

Chapter 8

Outeniqua

Tuesday 7 February

Wilderness

*W*e wake up and draw the curtains to an overcast morning, though warm. I make tea and empty the dishwasher. We must pack as we are leaving later in the day. S sends our daughter Lucy a text on my phone saying we are all right. Lucy replies that they are missing us and we have been away a long time.

We have breakfast on the deck under the bent and tangled trees; cereal and toast with fish paste. S decides to stay at home for the morning and read her book. She walks with me some of the way to the lagoon and then turns back. I check she knows the way home: from the street our house is shrouded in bush.

I carry on and meet Val and Stephen who have gone by car and are in the car park. I take pictures of the Syndicate houses on the front facing the lagoon, wondering whether the gabled one is the du Plessis cottage. I walk across the expanse of beach and wade the river mouth where a stream of brown water is running into the sea at low tide. Val and Stephen are exploring the rocks at the far end of the beach where the rough sea is tamed by a jutting craggy promontory. The water is too cold for swimming and the rocks too sharp to walk on so we decide to go back to the lagoon.

On the way we meet Sid and Erica wading in the river mouth. We go to the lagoon and swim. It is shallow and cool, the brandy coloured water mixed with a little tidal salt water. We find a deep part and relax in the water, making small talk. The women swim a little way off and have their own chat. The sky is bright overcast and it is pleasantly quiet with no cares. This is one of the best dips I've had, semi-warm, semi-salt. We dry off, put on sandals and drive back to the cottage. S has been getting on with Leonie, a woman who comes to clean the house.

While we were out Leonie alerted S to a monkey sitting in a chair on the deck, but by the time S looks out she sees only its back as it leaves, jumping into the branches of the trees. I have still not seen the loerie bird, though have often heard its deep frog like call inside the greenery.

We pack our bags and I arrange them in the back of the car. We go to the Nature's Valley restaurant for lunch rather than finishing up leftovers in the house. We give these to Leonie for her lunch and S also gives her money.

At the pub we sit outside under the umbrellas and eat "Boogie Burgers". We go to Sid and Erica's house to say our farewells. Erica wants our email address and we are already on hug and kiss terms when we say goodbye.

It is a short drive to Plettenberg Bay where we visit the famous Beacon Isle Hotel perched on a rock surrounded by beach and sea and accessible by a causeway. It used to be the site of a whaling station. The hotel has a beach beside it and Guy once spent the whole day in the water here when he was little. I used to be a guest of Hal and Peggy, friends of my parents, when they had a holiday cottage in Plettenberg Bay. We will be visiting Peggy in the town of Prince Albert tomorrow: she is 92 and lives in an old age home. The hotel and beach have changed little, though Plettenberg Bay's main Lookout Beach was largely swept away by the 2005 flooding of the Keurbooms River.

S and I look at the shops, then we leave "Plett" and drive towards Knysna where we stop at a roadside stall called Elephant Walk. The wares are good. S buys a handmade African doll for granddaughter Amelie and I get a cute T-shirt for grandson George with a zebra "earning its stripes" for South Africa.

We pull into Wilderness, our next overnight stop. It has a big lagoon that lies behind a spit of land that separates it from the ocean. The lagoon is surrounded by houses with prime water views. The inlet is formed by the barrier of sand banks on the beach that dam the Touw River. It is enclosed by reed beds inhabited by hundreds of birds. This is where my second cousin Hugo Leggatt and his wife Helen live, in a house called *Birdhaven*. We pull into the driveway. Helen is there, but I have not seen her for so long, I do not immediately recognise her. She is saying goodbye to her son Michael who has children in the car. There is much greeting and cheerful banter.

Helen and Hugo are in their 70s but look younger. They show us to our room which has a balcony overlooking the lagoon. Upstairs are additional spacious rooms also looking over water: a balcony, living room, dining room and kitchen. It is warm enough to sit out for tea and then all evening. Hugo inherited the house from his parents. He was an only child and spent his career teaching maths and science at South Africa's top private schools, Michaelhouse and Bishops. They have two sons beside Michael – Christopher and the eldest Nick, a committed sailboat enthusiast who takes part in round the world yacht races.

We talk family and look at old photo albums. Hugo's father and mine were cousins. Hugo tells me that our common great grandfather Samuel Leggatt had a brother, Horatio. They married sisters called Stedman and owned adjoining farms near Fareham in Hampshire, outside Portsmouth. Between them they produced 20 children in the early Victorian period (1840-50). Horatio's line of descendants came to an end with the death of the last male heir in an aircraft accident in 1931. Samuel's line carried on with the grandfathers of Hugo and me.

Today great grandfather Samuel's line of male succession lies with my sons, Guy and Roger, and with Hugo's three sons. My eldest son Guy and his wife Marnie in Alberta have produced two sons, Max and Joe, who now form the Canadian contingent. Two of Hugo's sons, Michael and Christopher, have between them produced three boys to carry on the name. My younger son Roger is due to marry his fiancé Emily this year, so they represent the possibility of starting a branch of the Leggatt line in Vancouver.

The two boys who live next door with Christopher – Julian and Luke – come over to greet us. They are lovely confident boys. Hugo's eldest, Nick, is unmarried. He is so wedded to a life of sailing that he told his father: "I have had such a good upbringing I don't want children unless I can give them the same." As we visit, Nick is taking part in a yacht race round the world with his partner Phillippa. Their yacht *Phesheya* (Zulu for "Overseas") is in the south-east Pacific somewhere between New Zealand and Cape Horn. Helen is feeling stressed because they have problems with weather and equipment and are being carried in the wrong direction by wind and wave. She follows Nick and Phillippa on the race website which shows the position of each yacht and its heading, and where daily updates are posted. She is constantly consulting the website.

At this point (although later they overcame their difficulties) Helen, the eternal mother, just wants Nick to go back to New Zealand and fly home and give up sailing. Hugo says more philosophically, "Oh well, he's enjoying himself, it's what he wants to do." He seems more worried about the cost as Nick did not attract full sponsorship for the race. "But if they make it," says

Hugo brightly, "they will become the first South Africans to complete that race and Pip the first woman to do so."

Helen has made a one pot meal which we serve ourselves. She is an animated, direct person who speaks her mind. She makes it clear she is not planning to sit up all night politely chatting to her guests. This suits us all. Helen is Greek and was brought up in Uganda where her father was a businessman and owned the Coca-Cola bottling plant. She has had a colourful life: as a young woman she was one of the first women racing car drivers. Formal wedding pictures taken in Uganda show Hugo and Helen as a very handsome couple. Now she is called "Yiayia" by her grandchildren, the Greek word for Granny. Hugo started his working life in London working for a firm which made specialised bulbs for the instrument lights of the Concorde supersonic passenger jet, lights that would be superseded by liquid-crystal displays.

When the others go, Hugo invites me to view his family archives on the computer. He is an expert on Leggatt family history and has pictures of our ancestors, dozens of documents and family trees about who was who and what they did. He goes on Google Earth to show me what he found last year when he visited a village called Crofton, near Fareham, where the churchyard has a number of Leggatt graves.

Adjoining the church a house he thinks is Crofton Manor where the family portrait I have on my bedroom wall was taken in about 1906. The photograph, taken outdoors on a special occasion, shows my Dad, Max, age about six, his mother, May, and father Samuel, a clergyman, and two baby sisters, Betty and Barbara; as well as Hugo's Dad, Desmond, Hugo's grandfather, Charles and other relatives. The portrait shows a stern Aunt Et (Ethel) who never married as she devotedly looked after her mother into her 90s, Uncle Norman, who later farmed at Westminster where I grew up in the Free State province of South Africa, and Uncle Frank Leggatt, an English shipping agent whose son Guy, another cousin of my father's, lived at both Westminster and Wilderness.

Just as the Crofton/Fareham area in Hampshire was a centre for the Leggatts in England, so Wilderness became the same in South Africa. Aunt Et, Norman and his wife Dora, and Frank, all lived in Wilderness, attracted no doubt by the beautiful setting and the kind climate. It was to Wilderness that Hugo's parents came to join the other Leggatts in the winter of 1946-47, one of the coldest of the century in England, underscoring the deprivation of the post-war years.

Hugo was six and was left in England while his father Desmond and mother Sylvia went out to Wilderness for a visit. Desmond was a barrister at the Old Bailey and had escaped war service. Although still in work he bought a property in Wilderness, came back to England, collected Hugo, and returned to Wilderness to live, arriving in November 1947. S and I stayed with Desmond and Sylvia on our pre-natal holiday in 1972. They lived on a hilltop overlooking Wilderness and owned only a boathouse on the lagoon, which was later converted into the house we are now staying in.

Hugo says Norman Leggatt, brother of my grandfather, was a British soldier who fought in the South African War and stayed on after the peace in 1902. He has Norman's South African War medal inscribed "Sergeant Leggatt". My father Max was sent from England by the family to work for his Uncle Norman in Westminster in about 1918. He would have been age 18 and he never returned to England. The farming district he went to was founded by the richest man in England, the second Duke of Westminster, Hugh Richard Arthur Grosvenor, known as Bendor after his father's racehorse, a Derby winner in 1880. The Duke was an officer in the war on the staff of Lord Milner, the British High Commissioner. Milner followed a policy of "Anglicisation" to achieve British dominance over the defeated Boers.

With wealth derived from ownership of valuable freehold property in central London, the Duke was persuaded by Milner to invest in a project of settling British subjects on farms in the Free State as part of Anglicisation. The Duke bought extensive lands, built himself a manor house, and divided the area into 18 farms centred on a village and railway station named Westminster. The farming families came over from the Duke's Eaton Estate in Cheshire. The attractive sandstone manor house and gabled farmhouses, which are still in use today, were designed by the leading imperial architect Herbert Baker, who created the government buildings in Pretoria and New Delhi.

Norman, fresh from the war, is believed to have been one of the original managers, working on one of the farms. My father took the same path, working as a farm manager, until he met and married my mother Wendy. Her father, my maternal grandfather, Edward Dunstan, a Cornish Methodist missionary to the Transvaal and canny investor in South African mining and industrial stocks, was able to put up the capital for my father to buy his own farm at Westminster, where I grew up with my two siblings – Peter, my elder brother, a scientist and mathematician, and Val, my younger sister.

Hugo tells me with amusement of a remark my father made to him when he visited him in Westminster. It revealed his feelings towards the Afrikaners, an attitude typical of the time, when he said of someone: "I thought he was quite a nice chap, then I heard him talking Afrikaans."

Wednesday 8 February

Prince Albert

The famous February 8 has arrived, the date I set in an exchange of letters with Peggy Clow-Wilson to visit her in Prince Albert. She is a lady from my childhood who lived in Westminster and whose son Howard was my friend at Rhodes University. I also keep in touch with her younger son Mick who lives in Newmarket, England. I have swapped Christmas cards with Peggy for years and at some point I resolved to go out of my way to visit her when I was in South Africa.

I phoned Peggy last night to say when we would be coming. She sounded organised and was fully expecting us. She said the weather is extremely hot, the hottest of the year. We set 2.30pm as our expected arrival time and she was pleased as it suited her schedule. She said Howard, who stays in the same home, is not well.

Hugo and Stephen debated last night which was the best route to take over the mountains to Prince Albert, a town in the arid interior called the Karoo. There is the Swartberg Pass that is unpaved and more direct, and Meiringspoort which is paved and a longer way round. The difference between a "pass" and a "poort" is that the first goes over the mountains, the latter goes along valleys and defiles through them. Both compete for spectacular scenery and views. This is apparently one of the most beautiful and mountainous parts of South Africa which I have not seen before. We decide to take the longer, safer route of Meiringspoort.

We pack and get ready. It is raining a misty rain that Val says is typical of Wilderness. When they camp here it is not wet enough to stay inside but it is damp enough to spoil everything. Rather like England, I reflect, maybe it made the Leggatts feel more at home. We fill with petrol and Stephen checks the tyres. We leave the main N2 road just before the town of George and cut across farming country with hops and orchards, travelling towards the mountains. We are heading for the Outeniqua, a name derived from the indigenous word for "man laden with honey". Today the man and his honey are lost in the overcast but as we start ascending the Outeniqua Pass we look down on green fields behind us.

Unfortunately, higher up the route the views are obscured by fog all the way. We twist and turn up the pass, often obstructed by heavy lorries on the single carriageway gradient. Over the pass, the fog lifts but it is still overcast and grey. We are in the Little Karoo and it is dry and mountainous, reminding me of Nevada in the US.

We pass through Oudtshoorn, a town known for ostrich farming and the Cango Caves, dramatic limestone caverns, which are nearby. We take the road to Beaufort West and stop at a village, De Rust, for groceries to make a picnic. We enter Meiringspoort, a passage through the Swartberg mountains that takes us deeper inland to the Great Karoo.

We stop at a spotlessly kept picnic facility with an African attendant who is listening to his iPod. Later we stop again at a similar facility with *rondavels* (round thatched huts) with displays of the construction of Meiringspoort pass. A short walk takes us to a high waterfall with a thin silver stream in a fold of the mountains. Its height reminds me of the waterfall on Howe Sound on the way to Squamish outside Vancouver.

Meiringspoort displays remarkable evidence of the Earth's geology; extensive areas of folded sandstone rock, once the bed of shallow seas, line the road and scale the mountainsides. The rocks are craggy and arranged in fantastic patterns, often coloured with green lichen. Once out of the pass we pick up speed for Prince Albert. The road runs through country ornamented with hills and mountains that are beautiful in their aridity, their indigo shapes set against the blue sky.

Suddenly we are entering Prince Albert. We follow the directions Peggy gave me on the phone to turn at the Dutch Reformed Church in Pastorie Street and we pull up outside Huis Kweek Vallei, the old age home. Val and Stephen decide to go on to check into our guest house, the Observatory.

The heat of the day is intense after the air conditioned car. All complaints about cool weather after leaving Cape Town fall away. We ring the bell at the gate and it is released to let us in. We ask for Peggy and a woman in uniform with red epaulettes takes us down a cool dark corridor. Suddenly behind me, silhouetted against the glare of daylight coming through the door at the other end of the passage, is a figure in a wheelchair calling for me. I initially think it is a case of mistaken identity, but the figure persists in waving and calling until I have to go and see who it is. I was expecting Howard to be with Peggy but this is he, though after more than 40 years I scarcely recognise him.

He has something for me, a sheet of paper bearing a cartoon he has drawn. It has his trademark "CLow" signature on the corner, a play on his surname Clow-Wilson and the signature of the British cartoonist of distant memory, David Low. At Rhodes University, Howard drew cartoons for the student newspaper and was editor of a joke-filled fund-raising magazine *Rhodent* sold at the annual student carnival. A motorcycle accident in his early 20s which shattered his leg changed his life for good and his latest illness is a legacy of this old injury. Drawing and writing remain his link with a happier past and are a form of therapy.

I tell him I want to see Peggy first and will return to him. I go back to where S and the nurse are waiting and we enter Peggy's room. She looks well, slim and upright, on top form and full of smiles to see us. Her room is kept cool with an electric fan. She sits in an armchair in the middle of the room facing a television. The walls are full of pictures of family, her youngest son, Mick, in his graduation gown and only daughter Patricia and her boys when they were young. Patricia, who built up her own public relations agency, tragically died of cancer at the age of 33.

We talk about our trip, about family, about the past in Westminster, and Peggy's life in Prince Albert. Her husband Hal decided on the move from Plettenberg Bay to Prince Albert as he loved the clear dry climate of the Karoo. Not long after the move he died of prostate cancer. Peggy remains cheerful and positive. She stands out as the only English-speaking person in the home. She says she objects to being referred to as "that Englishwoman". She corrects them by saying she is an English-speaking South African. Though born in South Africa, England was her finishing school. She danced at the Savoy and lived in a manor house with Hal who was a farmer. Now she is left with her memories in this beautiful but remote Karoo town.

I go back and sit with Howard in his room. He has a Rhodes University publication on his dresser and a blue plastic envelope from which he shows me samples of his drawing and writing. Our conversation verges on the incoherent. I say "Remember when we hitch-hiked to Cape Town as students?" His face lights up at the memory but his subsequent comments are about something else. The cartoon he gave me shows a person in bed in hospital, a situation unfortunately painfully familiar to him, with the nurse bringing food. The caption reads "No thanks! I'll have the fillet with creamed potato, salad and mushrooms. Then chocolate mousse – not the diabetic one either". It seems to reveal a poignant longing for a normal life.

I go back to Peggy. She and S are still in animated conversation. After a while Peggy asks where we go next on our trip and when we are leaving for England. We take the hint and end the visit. Peggy gets up with her stick, goes out to her electric wheelchair in the corridor, hangs her stick on the railing and drives out to see us off at the gate. She looks self-possessed and cheerful as we wave and turn away.

S and I walk in the heat towards the white-washed church with its impressive clock spire and turn left as Peggy instructed us. We come to the street where the guest house is located but can't identify it. I call Val on my cellphone, and Stephen comes to pick us up in the car. The guest house is comfortable, with a pool, a green shaded garden with guava and orange trees and gravelled walks. Stephen shows us the irrigation channels that lead water to each garden in the street. A freshwater crab scuttles along in the clear, shallow stream that comes in under the garden wall and goes out to the next garden.

Inside, the house has high ceilings and it is cool and dark with stained wood flooring and luxurious rooms. It is owned by Belgian people who come to Prince Albert to study the stars. The garage has been converted to an observatory with the roof sliding away to give the telescopes a clear view. It is padlocked but we can see the array of telescopes through the window.

S and I have a room with a four poster bed draped with a mosquito net. We change to go for a swim, cool off, then drink beer and talk on the veranda under the grape vines. Although we have a well equipped kitchen, we go out to dinner at a steak house in the town. The architecture of Prince Albert, set out on a series of grid-pattern streets, is quite striking; neatly built, solid bungalows with metal roofs; freshly painted, often in white with colour flashings; wrought-iron decoration on shady front verandas, all redolent of the Victorian era. The steak house is friendly and hospitable. There is a veranda but the evening is cool and we share the inside room with several other diners, including families with babies and young children.

When we leave to drive back to the guest house a full moon is rising into an inky sky. Back at the house we study the stars without the benefit of our observatory. The stars are bright but do not seem as numerous as the northern sky. We can just make out the Southern Cross but the stars are faint and difficult to string together.

At 2am in the morning S and I are awake. We can hear the annoying whine of mosquitoes that are evidently inside the net. We put on the light and catch most of them, leaping about and clapping the palms of our hands together. The exercise is not conducive to returning to sleep. I put on the ceiling fan because we are hot. "I'd like to be back in nice cool Farnham," says S.

Thursday 9 February

Matjiesfontein

Dawn is early and the sun comes up about 6.30am. It will be another hot cloudless day. The mosquitoes are still flitting about. We walk to breakfast at a place round the corner called La-di-Da which advertises Breakfast, Lunch and Coffee. We are the only customers in a bright semi-outdoor area overlooking lawns and a pond on one side and the street on the other. Opposite is a handsome Cape Dutch gabled house dated 1896. We discover guava juice, a delicious pink fruit nectar, a refreshing foil for bacon and eggs.

As is often customary in South Africa we can't get away without chatting to the proprietor about where we are from and where we are going and getting some helpful tips for the day. We go back to the guest house and tidy up and pack. Val calls the agent for us to check out. He soon arrives and we chat to him in the shade of a tree in the street. The temperature is already about 30C.

We set off in the car in search of an olive farm we have heard about. It processes its olives into preserves and olive oil. We find it with some difficulty as there is no signage and we have to stop and ask people beside the road. The plant and buildings are all brand new so they must be just starting the business. The lady gives us olive oil to taste. It is distinctive and delicious and we buy a supply to take home to England with us.

We set off again on our way through the Great Karoo to our next stop, Matjiesfontein. The landscape is arid semi-desert, mountainous and carpeted with low shrubs, grey with bright blotches of yellow. When we reach the N1 national road, the main trunk route between South Africa's largest cities Johannesburg and Cape Town, there is remarkably little traffic. Much of it is wide single carriageway. They do not have inter-city, dual carriageway motorways in South Africa, but the roads are very good with well maintained surfaces.

You see groups of workers in the middle of nowhere meticulously grooming the road edges with strimmers and mowers even though there is not much vegetation to tend. Perhaps it makes sense in a country with high unemployment to offer jobs that keep people busy. As a result everywhere is immaculate, from rest stops to sidewalks, public spaces and gardens. And there is no litter.

At Laingsburg we stop for a break and to stretch our legs. Val tells us that in 1981, just after we had left South Africa for Vancouver, much of Laingsburg was carried away in a flood of biblical proportions. At the time Val, who was pregnant with Marian, plus Stephen and his then bachelor brother Anthony, were on a camping trip to a Karoo town called Graaff Reinet, further upcountry. At Laingsburg they stopped for petrol and also bought lamb chops for a barbecue.

It was raining hard and continued to rain until they reached Graaff Reinet. Next morning on the news they heard that Laingsburg was no more: the normally dry river had flooded the town and destroyed everything in its path. They never got the bill for the petrol they bought and they ended up eating chops from a butchery that no longer existed. Val said a friend back home was watching the news on TV and searching for a picture of their little green car being tossed on the raging waters, but they had escaped. We see a sign on the median indicating the high water mark of the flood.

After Laingsburg, it is a short drive into Matjiesfontein, a huddle of white-washed buildings against the backdrop of a hump-backed mountain in the distance off the main road. We arrive in a village that is no more than a railway station and a hotel resort. The Lord Milner Hotel has elaborate wrought iron balconies, and turrets like a Foreign Legion fort flying the British and South African flags. We check in and get grand high-ceilinged, panelled rooms with balconies big enough for a game of tennis, overlooking the square and the railway.

Matjiesfontein, 195 miles from Cape Town, was already a railway station when James Logan, a Scottish entrepreneur, gained the refreshment room concession in 1883, before the days of dining cars. Prospering on the heavy passing trade going from the Cape to the diamond fields of Kimberley and later the gold mines of the Rand, he built it into a Victorian health and holiday resort where visitors came to enjoy the clear Karoo air, believing it to be a bracing cure for the chest ailments of the damp British climate.

During the South African War it was a British remount camp quartering 10,000 troops and 20,000 horses. Today the Lord Milner Hotel continues the Victorian tradition with an old fashioned British feel, servants in Victorian frilly black and white dresses, English military prints on the walls, lots of wood and brass, low slung cast iron garden chairs of the kind in Victorian family portraits, a dress code in the dining room and large sumptuous rooms. Strangely, our bathroom has two normal size baths joined side by side in the middle of the room. It seems a pity to bath one at a time in only one of them.

It is not bathtime yet so we go in search of the swimming pool, which is not as easy as it sounds. After several false starts requiring trips back to Reception we find it is across a dry river bed through some attractive gardens where a man is mowing the lawn, past a frog pond we initially thought was meant to be the pool, to a place on the furthest edge of the property where the scrub begins. The pool is large, the water not quite pristine, salt rather than chlorine, but very cool and refreshing in the burning sunlight. The paving round the pool is too hot to walk on barefoot. There is a striking eucalyptus tree overlooking the pool old enough to have sheltered the troops, maybe the Australian contingent.

We have heard there is a good museum off the station platform and that a train will be passing at about 3.30pm. The railways seem to be like the roads, not very busy and a train passing through is an event. We look through the museum, a collection of artefacts of some interest. An empty goods train comes rumbling through. S and I go to the coffee shop for tea and buy some Karoo honey to take home with us. We return to our large cool rooms, and relax before dinner.

We meet in the pub beside the hotel, named the Laird's Arms after the founder Jimmy Logan. The pub is completely empty save for the barman and a rotund jolly fellow in a bowler hat who greets us and is the pub pianist. Earlier he had taken Val and Stephen on a ten minute tour of Matjiesfontein in an old red London bus. He is obviously on the make for tips and offers us a tour of the grand rooms at the back of the hotel that are not used but are shown to visitors. After we have enjoyed pints of beer, he invites us to stand round the piano and sing *She's Coming Round the Mountain* with him, which has conveniently repetitive words so we can sing along.

He cheerfully puts the banknotes we give him under his bowler hat and we go to dinner. We were probably his only punters all evening. In England I complain of too many people jamming up the works. Here there are too few. Everywhere customers are sparse, except of course in the cities like Cape Town. There are millions of potential customers out there, but they are too poor to fill the roads, the pubs, hotels and resorts. Maybe it is busier in the holiday season, but I hope one day the economy will expand to include a thriving indigenous class with the money and opportunity to enjoy what we lucky travellers take for granted.

Dinner is by candlelight. It is quite atmospheric but again we need more people in the room to give it a buzz. We have Karoo lamb chops, and the waitress in Victorian uniform dishes up five kinds of vegetables one by one from a silver platter she holds in one hand, with the other hand expertly manipulating a fork and spoon to serve us, like the footmen in *Downton Abbey*. By the time we are interested in dessert the dining room is empty and the serving staff have deserted us. We have to call out for service. Then I remember we are on African time.

Friday 10 February

Cape Town

My first peek through the curtains seems to reveal an overcast sky, but it is only the grey ceiling of the vast balcony outside the French doors. Beyond the wrought iron railing, the Karoo is still, the mountains opposite glowing softly, with the brightening sun promising another hot day. A security guard who watches guests' cars at night crunches along in the gravel parking area. A bird calls on one side, poop-poop-poop, and is answered further away on the other side, poop-poop-poop. It is very peaceful and far from any action.

Breakfast is an indulgent feast. Off the dining room is another large space with big bowls of tinned fruit in light syrup on one side, healthy breakfast choices of cereal, freshly baked brown bread and yoghurt on another, a table of jams and preserves, and a cooked breakfast station on the fourth side. This is the hot side where a woman in uniform cooks eggs to order over a gas burner in a large receptacle brimming with hot cooking oil.

With glasses of guava juice on the side, I have guava pieces, pears and watermelon to start, missing out the peaches, mixed fruit salad and prunes. At the hot buffet I order two fried eggs that are cooked while I serve myself sausages, bacon, mashed chicken livers (very rich) and a fritter of uncertain provenance which is later the only thing left unfinished. Then there is toast and home made marmalade. The meal is a highlight of the trip and sustains me the whole day until supper time.

We pack up and are soon back on the N1 heading for Cape Town with Val at the wheel. It is a continuation of the barren but beautiful landscape, travelling an excellent broad road with very little traffic. The hills and mountains are mostly formed of upended sedimentary layers. These mountains, hills and outcrops parallel our direction of travel until we reach a new wall of mountains that seem to block our path.

The vegetation is changing and we see our first vineyards. Then the road plunges downward at Matroosberg (Sailor Mountain), a mile-high mounded summit that looms over us. We pass out of the interior basin and into the Hex River Valley. The mountains are imposing, as high as the Rockies in Canada where I was with my son Guy last year, and in their way more grand and interesting. Here a new valley opens, broad from mountain range to mountain range on opposite sides, the floor covered in a green carpet of grape vines ready for harvest.

These grapes are destined for supermarkets like Waitrose and Sainsbury's in the UK and other countries – Cape grapes for the table. They hang in large profuse bunches out of the sun under the vines' canopy of leaves. Even though we are going quite fast and my eyesight is not that great we can clearly see the large bunches of green grapes and the red, with labourers with plastic trays starting to bring in the harvest. This is the start of the picking season and it goes on until March.

We stop at a *padstal* (road stall) that Val recommends for dried fruit and other produce. I buy a small bottle of muscadel, a sweet dessert wine, and fig jam, while S stocks up on dried fruit and homemade biscuits for her work colleagues. We chat to the manageress at the till. She has a son in Sheffield, and says the other son is also going to England to consider moving there. I am not sure it is as easy as that anymore, but we don't say anything. She says her sons fear for the future of their children. I say I see a country of opportunity. She replies that it is if you are the right colour. She is surprisingly negative about South Africa. I suspect her political views stem from the old days and she believes the country has gone to the dogs under majority rule.

We reach the town of Worcester, commercial centre of the Breede (Broad) River wine growing region. The road bypasses the town but we see a massive shopping mall complex, hinting at a high degree of prosperity, probably based on the wine export trade. We turn into a petrol station to fill up. We get a warm welcome, as if we are the only car of the day. No fewer than five attendants in bright red coveralls gesticulate and jump in excitement in our path, waving us into a refuelling bay. One ascertains from Stephen what we want and jams the nozzle in the filler neck, then he joins the others: they wash all the car windows with soapy water, wipe them down and dry with wads of paper.

After Worcester we approach Du Toit's Kloof, another range of high blue mountains with steep bare rock slopes even more lofty and impressive than those around Matroosberg. Kloof is the South African word for a cleft in the mountains or hills. The *fynbos* is with us again so we are in the true Cape. The road used to form a bottleneck through the mountains linking the coastal plain of Cape Town with the interior. Now it is a dual carriageway with the opposing lanes on different routes high and low through the valleys.

The road comes to a tunnel 4.4km long under the mountains but we choose to take the old single carriageway two way road over the top so we can see the views. Baboons stroll around beside the road, oblivious of the cars. As we go Stephen points out where there are hiking trails, and discusses the walks and climbs he has accomplished in this his paradise.

Finally the panorama of the coastal plain appears and we look down on another green carpet of vines and forests extending into the haze, surrounding the wine-growing centres of Paarl and Stellenbosch. We soon rejoin the main N1 carriageway, seeing the impressive viaduct that takes cars to the tunnel mouth on the Paarl side of the Du Toit's Kloof mountains. Then it is the rather dull run across the Cape Flats towards the coast and Cape Town.

The "Mother City" as Cape Town is sometimes called, has sprawled north considerably. Previously separate towns and suburbs are now all joined up in a jumble: Brackenfell, Durbanville, Tygerberg. As we near the city and see the cranes of the docks there is an impressive new business district in the manner of an English business park, Century City, with ranks of large office blocks and a sprawling shopping centre with cinemas and restaurants where Capetonians go for recreation when it is raining.

Back in the suburbs below the mountain, Stephen drops us with our bags, more numerous now, at the gate of Cape Paradise Lodge. Marco answers the buzzer and carries our bags. He also delivers the big suitcases that we stored in his garage. It is still early afternoon. The weather has turned cool and cloudy. S wants to see Serengeti, the block of furnished apartments in the suburb of Gardens not far away where we stayed when our daughter Lucy was born in 1976.

We get ready and set off down the hill, with a communal mini-van taxi trying to pick us up. We give it the slip and walk across De Waal Park to Breda Street. Serengeti is so changed as to be almost unrecognisable. Heavy duty security gates, warning notices and electric wires are in place. I used to drive in off the street after work without impediment. S stood for hours in the night rocking baby Lucy to sleep in her arms while walking the floor and watching the winking lights of the advertising signs over the city.

At the nearby shopping centre, we buy the *Cape Argus*, the evening paper, to take home and read. As we step into the street it starts to rain in a fine mist so we return to take a taxi. He charges R40 (£4) and we tip him R10 (£1). I suspect it is a pirate taxi as it is dirty and where a meter should be are bare wires sticking out of the dash. But the lettering on the door claims it is a taxi and gives an hourly fare. By the time we have gone a few yards it has already stopped drizzling.

We change and go to dinner at Bacini's, then read the paper. President Jacob Zuma has made a speech at the opening of Parliament, which is now called the State of the Nation Address. He announces a financial plan to help people buy houses and another to boost infrastructure projects. The Democratic Alliance opposition party wonder whether the spending will be sufficiently controlled to ensure delivery of projects without money being misappropriated.

Another report says bulldozers are returning to District Six, not this time to destroy, but to build 1,000 houses by 2014 in restitution of those removed 30 or more years ago under apartheid. A claimant aged 68 says he was born in District Six and hopes to have a house there again before he dies.

The *Cape Argus* is owned by an Irish company, Independent News & Media, now the largest newspaper publisher in South Africa. It also owns the *Independent* in London. My reporter friend Chris at Agulhas told me they bought the Argus Group – of which my paper *The Star* was part – for a knock down price reflecting the mood at the end of white rule. The package included all the cover titles and buildings, printing plants and other assets. S reads it and says it is just as well I moved on when I did.

It rains intermittently in the night, a light rushing sound. Now we have had all Cape Town weather: roaring gales, burning sunshine and cooling rain.

Cape glory - seen from the Silvermine Nature Reserve,
the Peninsula town of Hout Bay.

Nelson Mandela's cell in which he was
imprisoned for 18 years on Robben Island.

The Pebble Beach guest house at Cape Agulhas.

Prime holiday real estate - the Syndicate houses
line the lagoon front at Nature's Valley.

Nature's Valley township hemmed in between
the Tsitsikamma Nature Reserve and the sea.

Days gone by - the Lord Milner Hotel
at Matjiesfontein near Cape Town.

Wine farm - the Cape Dutch gabled manor house
at Groot Constantia outside Cape Town.

Family tree - A gathering of Leggatts, perhaps at Crofton,
Hampshire in 1906. Hugh's father Max, age six, sits
on the ground at his mother May's knee (left). Behind,
standing, is father Samuel, Hugh's grandfather.

End game - executives of the Canadian gold mining company
Placer Dome meet President Nelson Mandela in Johannesburg
in 1999. Brett Kebble is centre right and Hugh behind.

Cape Town family - Val and Stephen, centre, with their children,
Simon, left, with Michela, and Marian, right, with Luke.

Chapter 9

Flyaway

Saturday 11 February

Cape Town

We wake up to rain, but it soon clears. Later the clouds and cool damp return, making it a rogue weather day for our outing with friends. S goes out to make tea in the dining area and meets Patricia waiting to give the guests their breakfast. It is her last day before we leave so S gives her some money. I get a super generous portion at breakfast.

We get ready to be picked up by Hans and Tessa to go to lunch in the winelands. They are friends since the days we lived at Serengeti in Breda Street where S met Tessa in the lift, both clutching newborns. S and Tessa are both British so they also had that in common. We see Hans and Tessa almost every year when they visit England to see their children who have left South Africa.

Hans, who lives in Tokai, an outer suburb, and does not have much occasion to drive into central Cape Town, needs directions to put us on the N2 highway to Somerset West. He takes us to a wine farm called Avontuur (Adventure). The women sit at the back and exchange news so I talk with Hans in the front about the situation in South Africa.

I discuss what I picked up on from the opening of Parliament. He ruefully describes how government money seems to disappear down black holes. "We don't have to look into space for black holes, we have them right here," he quips. Looking at the mixture of state built and shanty housing along the side of the highway, he is pessimistic about South Africa ever catching up with demand for housing. Some families living in a shanty are given a house for free under the Restitution Development Plan (RDP). Often in such a situation the house is rented out for income and the family builds another shanty in the yard. "The authorities condemn the practice, but do not do anything about it," says Hans.

South Africa has the most developed economy in Africa, which attracts migrants from the rest of the continent – the honeypot effect. The Government refuses to control its borders as it regards these migrants as coming from states that "supported the struggle" in the years of apartheid. So the outsiders, like the man from Congo that I met at Muizenberg, take housing and jobs from

South Africans. I suggest the borders of South Africa are so long that attempts to seal them as they attempt to in North America would fail anyway.

Avontuur has a wine tasting room where we are offered hospitality. Hans likes the rosé wine and arranges to buy some. At lunch I have another huge meal, of chicken livers on toast with a Thai curry sauce, followed by more Karoo lamb chops, the third time in four days.

We drive back to Cape Town. At the big bend on De Waal Drive by Groote Schuur Hospital an accident has taken place on the opposite carriageway. In the slanting sunlight a mass of stopped cars across seven lanes gleam with impatience. I suggest Hans take the longer route over Kloof Nek back to their home in Tokai to avoid the gridlock. We say our farewells and suggest we reciprocate when they are next in England. Back at the guest house the weather is grey and gloomy and S wants some exercise after lunch and sitting in the car. We go up on to the trails on the lower slopes of Table Mountain.

We decide to call on Val and Stephen, especially as I can see Devil's Peak veiled in rain and it is coming nearer along the top of Table Mountain. We are damp when we get there. Marian is visiting and so are Simon and Michela. They are working with Val to upholster an ottoman for Simon's apartment. We are invited to stay for supper but decline after our big lunch. We say our goodbyes and Simon drives us back to the guest house. Both of us feel we are ready to return home. "It will be nice to be able to eat our own food again," says S.

Sunday 12 February

Cape Town

We often have cloud over Table Mountain, the usual when the south-easter is blowing, but today the cloud is over Table Bay and the mountain is clear. This means the north-west airflow that brought yesterday's showers is still in charge.

After breakfast we meet Marco and he suggests we settle the bill for our stay as he will be out for most of the day. He is entertaining family who are visiting from Germany. We go down to his flat and pay R7,600 (£648.31) for eight nights' accommodation including breakfast, which we think is reasonable for the comfort, convenience and hospitality.

Val and Stephen pick us up. We go over Kloof Nek and head down to Camps Bay. I am checking my receipt from the guest house and find I have left my credit card with Marco: it was still in the machine when we left as we were talking too much. I call Marco. He has the card and will put it in our room.

We drive through Hout Bay and on to the Chapman's Peak road. It is a bright crisp morning made clear and cooler by the north-westerly and the rain. Cape Peninsula recreation is on full display. Hundreds of cyclists swarm the sides of the roads in both directions. Many have mountain bikes but most have the road bikes with narrow tyres. All these young people are making the best of their fantastic climate and getting out and enjoying themselves. We see football games, horse riding and hikers revelling in the sun-drenched setting of mountain and sea.

On Chapman's Peak Drive overlooking Hout Bay we overtake Marian and her friend Claudine who are cycling up a hill. They are doing the circuit from central Cape Town and back through Simon's Town. Stephen knew it was likely we would see them. We pull into a viewpoint and they follow on their bicycles and we have a chat. They are so physically fit that they are not even puffing; they do not seem to have raised a sweat. Marian has form when it comes to extreme sports. She and Luke were among the few riders to complete a 4,000km cycle race down the Great Divide of North America from Banff in Canada to New Mexico in 2011. They have also scaled the Himalayas together, ascending a 6,500m peak (21,300ft).

We turn back and Marian and her friend continue cycling. We head over a saddle in the Peninsula mountain chain to Constantia, the oldest wine farm at the Cape, established by Dutch Governor Simon van der Stel in 1685. The car park is full and families with young children are enjoying their Sunday morning under green umbrellas beside the coffee shop. The manor house is a classic of Dutch gabled architecture and the lush surrounding vines produce wine and port.

The Kirstenbosch gardens are on the route back to Cape Town and S wants to do some last-day shopping there for family and friends. We are dropped off and Val and Stephen go to find parking, arranging to meet us at

Mandela's statue in the gardens. We buy guinea fowl-print tea towels, a matching tea cosy, books and cards. Once inside Kirstenbosch Val and Stephen walk us round part of the botanic gardens.

It is warm this side of Table Mountain, sheltered from the north-west air flow. Fernwood Peak, a buttress at the end of Table Mountain, and Devil's Peak at its side, soar serene and green over us. Families, groups and couples are lying about the green lawns having picnics; children play games. A band shell is set up beside a large lawned area and technicians are tuning loudspeakers ready for an outdoor evening concert. S volunteers to buy lunch and we find our way to the restaurant. We have a light meal before returning. It is time to start packing for our departure.

In the evening we dress and walk over to Glen Crescent for the last meal of our stay. Marian and Luke join us while Simon and Michela had a prior engagement. At dinner in the dining room we have roast gammon and vegetables.

Luke, who is a doctor in accident and emergency, tells us about a colleague who is studying sports science – the physiology of exercise and how to optimise physical performance. Studies have shown it is indeed "all in the mind". The brain controls everything. You can get all the mechanics right in the use of muscle and bone but if the brain doesn't direct higher performance you won't swim faster or run more swiftly. Interestingly, on the other hand, the brain won't let the body overdo it.

Luke turns to discussion of diet arising from the sport science. Studies have shown that because early humans were hunter gatherers, the best diet for them is protein and fat, not carbohydrates, which make up much of many people's diets today. As hunter gatherers there was little opportunity to consume carbohydrates as they came only from certain roots like potatoes, from sweet berries and a little from certain animal parts. Carbohydrates give people a fast energy fix but too much in combination with other factors can lead to obesity and diabetes. Obesity is often associated with poverty because carbohydrates are relatively inexpensive.

Luke says whatever you eat will only shift your cholesterol count by one unit. So if you have high cholesterol, cutting out fatty food like butter and sausages is not going to make a decisive difference. The liver produces cholesterol which is needed by blood cells. When S was ill and thin following her brain haemorrhage she had a higher cholesterol count than when she was well even though she was barely eating, so her body, because it was not getting cholesterol from food intake, was manufacturing it from the liver.

At the end of the meal we sadly say our good-byes. Stephen very kindly goes through the inconvenience of getting the car out in the dark to run us home. We will see him again in the morning when they pick us up for the airport.

In the night we have mosquitoes dive-bombing us again. I spray the room with a can of pesticide called Doom that I find in the closet and it seems to work.

Monday 13 February

London

We are awake before the alarm goes off at 4.45am. We have both slept fitfully. We wash and dress and finish packing. I take our three heavy bags downstairs as quietly as I can so as not to wake the other guests; rumble, rumble across the pine floors. In the half light, Val and Stephen are at the gate in the car. The three cases load easily into the back, standing up in a row like books on a shelf. I close the iron gates of Cape Paradise Lodge with the remote attached to our room keys and drop the bunch in the slot of the locked mailbox. Stephen drives to the airport through light early morning traffic and we are at the Departure level at 6am.

We thank Val and Stephen again for all their hospitality and for looking after us; Val is a bit teary. We all hug. A porter takes our bags on a trolley and delivers us to the correct British Airways queue. Check in, security and passport control all go smoothly. Security seems a bit casual, not as tight and focused as elsewhere; it is as if the personnel have been trained for the job but do not have a sense of the underlying purpose. Then passport control is pure Africa.

There are two woman officers in booths side by side divided by opaque glass so they are not in the same space. While checking passports and tapping keys on their computers they carry on an animated personal conversation. They are out of sight of one another and speak in loud Xhosa, one of the main African languages, the tongue of the sainted Mandela. No notice at all is taken of bemused passport holders as they chat and chortle away for all the world as if they are doing their knitting at home.

S is starting to feel faint from the early rising and needs a carbohydrate fix to raise energy levels. Once we are through passport control we head for a coffee shop. They are setting out delicious looking freshly made paninis and sandwiches but we stick with a muffin and croissant with coffee. Too late we spot the pink guava juice; we miss our last chance to have some. The muffin revives us and S feels better. She goes shopping for a gift for her 97-year-old mother and buys a picture book of Cape Town scenery. It is 7.15am and we are all done with jobs and ready to go. We get in the queue before they announce boarding.

We are on the Table Mountain side when we take off. The run-up gathers pace. Looking at the Old Grey Father reposing unconcerned, its top wreathed in cloud, slipping away behind with the forward motion of the aircraft, I suddenly get an unexpected pang of emotion, like leaving home for boarding school.

The heavily laden Boeing 747 lumbers off, the engines singing in overdrive as the aircraft hefts tons of people and luggage – Hex River peaches and bottles of jam, dirty shirts and gifts for grandchildren – up into the early morning sky. The shadow of the plane, too big to see when on the ground, gets smaller and smaller against the backdrop of fields and houses as the plane climbs higher. We fly over the coast of False Bay before banking to the right over the sea. I get a good bird's eye view of the spine of the Peninsula mountains running back from the bulk of Table Mountain towards Cape Point, cradling the concave flatlands of Retreat, Tokai and Constantia.

I trace the layout below me. There is Fish Hoek where we ate fish and chips and swam in the waves. Further along is Simon's Town where we watched penguins and took a dip at Boulders Beach. Then we cross the Peninsula and turn north, flying over the waters between Robben Island and Green Point where we watched the *QM2* sail away on the continuation of her world voyage.

We reach cruising altitude while we can still see Green Point and the city centre dwindling away behind us, the glare from the rising sun obscuring the detail. Val and Stephen have said they can follow the flights from their veranda. I had sent Val a message that we were taxiing so I wonder if she is watching.

The plane settles down to the long haul, we get out our books to read. People prefer the window blinds down to reduce the glare. Later I raise the blind to see and we are over the ocean off the west coast, a line of brown indentations. Then we lose sight of land and for the next few hours we stay over the South Atlantic, heading north towards the bulge of Africa.

We are 36,000ft above the sea. When the *QM2* traversed these waters we had at times 18,000ft beneath our keel. That means there is a 54,000ft envelope from ocean bottom to stratosphere through which we have floated and flown. Following the progress of the flight on the journey map at my seat, it takes five hours' of jetting to reach the equator from Cape Town; while going south it took the *QM2* five leisurely days from latitude zero to the Cape at 33S.

During the flight, time passes quickly. Meals are for the tummy, not to satisfy the palate. I read a book Val recommended and lent me called *Killing Kebble, an Underworld Exposed*, a true story about the death of a Johannesburg mining tycoon in the most extraordinary circumstances.

It is written by a Johannesburg *EyeWitness News* reporter, Mandy Wiener, who covered the case from the first crime scene. The book shines the spotlight on the magnate Brett Kebble and his shady business dealings. He acquired interests in major South African gold mining companies, Johannesburg Consolidated Investments (JCI) and Western Areas, by borrowing from Peter to pay Paul, taking shareholder funds from company coffers and leveraging complicated cross holdings through ownership of shell companies. Because of his wealth and evident business acumen, he was regarded as a hero of the business world. He was a staunch supporter of the new order in South Africa, handing out money to the ANC Youth League and generally occupying a respected place in society.

I was among those unsuspecting people when I briefly met Kebble 13 years ago on a visit to Johannesburg with Placer Dome, the mining company I worked for in Canada. In April 1999, six months before I left Placer Dome, the company, then under the leadership of a luckless chief executive called John Willson, bought a 50 per cent joint venture interest in a JCI-Western Areas gold project called South Deep outside Johannesburg. It was hailed as the first major investment by a foreign company in the South African gold mining industry. Placer Dome set up an office, assigned its best technical and managerial staff, set up systems that linked the business with Vancouver and generally put a lot of resources into it.

I was included in a group of executives led by the chairman Rob Franklin who flew to Johannesburg to mark the completion of the transaction. I was agog at the excitement of returning in the role of a foreign visitor to my homeland. In my guise of Canadian communications person we visited the offices of *The Star* to brief reporters about Placer Dome. The visit to Johannesburg included a black tie dinner and, exceptionally, a visit with then President Nelson Mandela at his home in Houghton, an upmarket residential suburb of Johannesburg.

This could well have been arranged by Kebble himself because we were all assembled at Kebble's home, also in Houghton, where I met him as part of the group while we waited for the President to summon us for a visit. I did not have a conversation with Kebble but I remember him as a joking, genial fellow in high spirits. Then we went to see the President, each of us shaking Mandela's hand in greeting as we arrived. I can still recall the silky smoothness of his hand.

In a 20-minute meeting sitting in his living room, Mandela told us he started working life as a mining company security guard and jokingly suggested that as he was about to retire as President of South Africa, Placer Dome might have a job for him. Afterwards an aide took a picture of us with the President. I later published it with an article in the corporate magazine. I was reminded of this only when looking at photo albums during our visit and Val produced the print I had sent her. This also prompted her to lend me the book to read.

I didn't follow what happened to South Deep because I lost interest in Placer Dome with my move to Rio Tinto in London. But after Barrick Gold took over Placer Dome in 2005, Barrick soon sold the stake off to a South African company, Gold Fields. South Deep is still under development, a technically difficult project more than 11,000ft below the surface, so I doubt whether the mine as an investment was all that it was cracked up to be. *Killing Kebble* mentions Kebble's need to sell off part of South Deep to get his hands on some cash, so with the benefit of hindsight Placer Dome may have been a little starry-eyed. After all, the company had a less than dazzling record of business investment. It lost money on a Soviet-era gold project in Kazakhstan, then, after South Deep, made an over-generous purchase of Getchell Gold in the US, all the while badly under-estimating the risk of a flagship gold project called Las Cristinas in Venezuela, which still lies undeveloped today.

Fast forward six years from 1999 to September 2005 and Kebble is facing ruin. As *Killing Kebble* tells it, he was in such a devastating financial state with all his holdings unravelling and Peter catching up with Paul that he became intent on suicide. He thought death was the only route out for him. Because he was held in high regard and wanted his reputation to remain intact, he sought to make his death look like an accident or, true to form in South Africa, a car hijacking. He even considered poisoning the pilot of his executive jet to cause a crash. However, happily for the pilot, Kebble's security people had links with the Johannesburg underworld of drug dealers, enforcers and nightclub bouncers, so three gangsters were hired by a security chief to stage an assassination.

In a comedy of errors, it took three attempts to do the deed. The first night, Kebble set off in his Mercedes to the appointed street, the gunmen following and flashing their lights to let Kebble know it was them. Then the gunmen's car overheated (apparently they had borrowed the wife's jalopy) so the hitmen had to turn away and go home, leaving Kebble driving around looking for the people who were meant to kill him and calling them on his cellphone.

Next night on the same street, the rendezvous was made again. This time on the first attempt, as the gunmen's car came alongside Kebble's Mercedes, with the driver's window down and Kebble looking at them with his near side shoulder raised as if to ward off the bullets, the revolver did not fire. Another circuit was made and the cars both came to a stop side by side but again the revolver did not fire. The gunmen drove off and on the third attempt, after emptying the cylinder and re-loading, the gun did go off and seven bullets killed

Kebble. It was a sensational crime story at the time, attracting international attention and going from grief and consternation at the murder of a prominent businessman to the later discovery he staged his own murder.

As if not already bad enough, the murder turned out to be the tip of an iceberg, as the subsequent investigations revealed that Kebble's links to the underworld included bribery of the South African police commissioner who was in the pay of Kebble's security people. While in Cape Town, I read in the *Cape Argus* that the ex-commissioner's appeal against his conviction for corruption had been refused.

Ultimately, although the killers were identified and the shooter tells his story at length in the book, no one was convicted of the murder of Kebble because of a bungled plea bargaining scenario by the prosecutors. It is a fascinating glimpse into the murky underworld of post apartheid South Africa. I am surprised that among all the gangsters and gunmen in the Kebble case, only one was a person of colour. I finish the book on the plane feeling slightly sick.

For fresh air I raise the blind to follow our route in tandem with the journey map on the video screen at my seat. We cross the coast of Africa near Accra in Ghana and head inland over the "bulge" of the African continent, a shortcut between the southern tip and Europe. In the years of apartheid, South African Airways had to stay out to sea and fly round the bulge because no African country would permit South Africa to use their air space. When the cloud cover over the equatorial region clears, I can see below us the semi-desert turning to the full desert of the Sahara. Fantastic patterns are traced in sand dunes on the surface of the Earth for thousands of miles.

We bypass Tamanrasset and Adrar in Algeria's vast hinterland and reach the Mediterranean coast near Algiers. The route then follows a lefthand arc up into France, over Marseilles and Paris into the London area, right on schedule at 5.45pm. The weather is clear and it is just getting dark as people go home after their Monday workday. London is an immense carpet of lights tracing the maze of streets and thoroughfares laid out in such an irregular and haphazard way this can only be England. I see the famous bridges and landmarks along the Thames as we approach Heathrow over West London. The landing is smooth and bump free; we're back.

In the terminal our luggage is efficiently retrieved; only a wagging sniffer dog is interested in what is in our bags, and it doesn't do dried fruit or Madeira wine. We soon meet our driver from Home James taxis in Farnham. He tells us we missed a cold spell with ice and snow. Now the weather is normal for February, 6deg and cloudy. S has the energy to talk to the driver on the way but I am mostly silent. I want to get home; from ship to shore and back again it has been a while.

Acknowledgements

The author acknowledges with thanks the use of brief quotations and references from these publications:

Harold Nicolson, *Journey to Java*. Constable and Company Ltd, London, 1957.

J B Priestley, *English Journey, Being a rambling but truthful account of what one man saw and heard and felt and thought during a journey through England during the autumn of the year 1933*. Penguin Books 1977. First published by William Heinemann Ltd 1934.

William Manchester, *A World Lit only by Fire, The Medieval Mind and the Renaissance, Portrait of an Age*. Little, Brown and Company (Canada) Limited 1992. ISBN 0-316-54531-7.

Richard Mullen and James Munson, *'The Smell of the Continent', The British Discover Europe*. Macmillan, London, 2009. ISBN 978-0-230-74190-4.

Anthony Delius, *The Last Division*. Human & Rousseau, Cape Town 1959.

Nora and Chris Sinclair, *The Story of Nature's Valley*. Print Afford, Plettenberg Bay, South Africa.

Mandy Wiener, *Killing Kebble, An Underworld Exposed*. Macmillan (South Africa) 2011. ISBN 978-1-77010-132-6.